'The journeys, struggles and insights of two great spiritual pilgrims – Ignatius Loyola and Mary Ward – are skilfully woven together here to invite today's pilgrims into their own Ignatian adventure. Gemma Simmonds' own knowledge and love of both of these wise guides shines through these pages as she offers us a map for our own journey that is deeply grounded, practical and *real*. An excellent and very readable companion through Lent, and far beyond.'

Margaret Silf, author and spiritual explorer

'Learning to pray by drawing on contemplation is vital today to be able to discern God's speaking through the details of our lives. To sustain a depth of faith in our challenging world, we need forms of prayer that maintain a rich and deeply nourishing spiritual life infused with the love of God. In this wonderful book, Gemma Simmonds explores and unpacks the method of prayer developed by St Ignatius in a way that makes the profound approach of the Jesuits accessible to those who want to be serious about their prayer lives. I highly recommend this book if you are hungry and seeking to encounter and discover God in a deeper way.'

Ian Mobsby, Anglican priest, writer, speaker and Prior, Wellspring
New Monastic Community, Peckham, London

'If you are looking for insightful and encouraging spiritual reading for Lent (or any other time), you have found your book! Grounding the spiritual in the practicable, Gemma Simmonds invites us to be pilgrims in the company of Jesus, Ignatius and Mary Ward. Learning from them along the way, we discover our own path to greater faith, hope and love.'

Kevin O'Brien SJ, author of The Ignatian Adventure: Experiencing
the Spiritual Exercises of Saint Ignatius in Daily Life, *and Dean,*
Jesuit School of Theology, Santa Clara University, California

D1082639

Dr Gemma Simmonds is Senior Lecturer in Pastoral and Social Studies and Theology at Heythrop College, University of London, where she teaches Ignatian spirituality. A sister of the Congregation of Jesus, she has worked in teaching and in university and prison chaplaincy, and has done missionary work among women and street children in Brazil. A renowned international speaker, Dr Simmonds is also a regular broadcaster on religious programmes and has been a spiritual director and retreat-giver since the 1990s.

THE WAY OF IGNATIUS

A prayer journey through Lent

Gemma Simmonds

First published in Great Britain in 2018

Society for Promoting Christian Knowledge
36 Causton Street
London SW1P 4ST
www.spck.org.uk

For copyright acknowledgements, see p. 89.

British Library Cataloguing-in-Publication Data
A catalogue record for this book is available from the British Library

ISBN 978–0–281–07531–7
eBook ISBN 978–0–281–07532–4

Typeset by Fakenham Prepress Solutions, Fakenham, Norfolk NR21 8NN
First printed in Great Britain by Ashford Colour Press

eBook by Fakenham Prepress Solutions, Fakenham, Norfolk NR21 8NN

Contents

Acknowledgements

Throughout my life from childhood I have been blessed with wise guides who have taught me how to speak with God 'as one friend speaks to another' through their own loving companionship.[1] I made my first Ignatian retreat aged 10 under the guidance of a Jesuit priest, Algy Shearburn SJ, and never looked back. I was educated by Mary Ward sisters who embodied so much that is best in the spiritual tradition that she shares with Ignatius Loyola and I am undyingly grateful to them, as to a long line of Jesuits and Ignatian lay people who, as spiritual guides, teachers, friends and colleagues have embodied in their teaching and their lives what I am writing about in these pages. I have had the privilege of teaching spiritual direction in the Ignatian tradition myself, and have had wonderful students from every Christian denomination and no determined faith at all. I have also enjoyed the even greater privilege of accompanying people on part of their lifelong spiritual journey, whether through retreats or weeks of guided prayer, regular spiritual companionship or as a university chaplain or prison volunteer. Their longing for ultimate meaning and connection, their struggles, curiosity, questions and challenges have taught me far more than they could ever imagine, so some of their wisdom also finds its way into this book.

The key figures in these groups are too many to be listed, but I am especially grateful to Pia Buxton, Armine Radley, Miriam Ybarra, Gillian Orchard and Cecilia Goodman, whom I was proud to call my sisters, to my colleagues Eddie Howells and David Lonsdale, and to Kathleen McGhee SND, Kathryn Fitzgerald, Barb Weigand, George Aschenbrenner SJ and the staffs of St Beuno's and the Jesuit Center for Spiritual Growth in Wernersville, Pennsylvania, who were generous enough to teach me what they knew of the craft of accompanying others in the footsteps of Ignatius.

1

Getting going

Discovering what we already have

———◆———

We're here because we're here.[1]

This is emphatically not a book for experts or, indeed, a book by an expert on prayer or the spiritual life. I'm not sure what such experts would look like, since I have never met any. I have met a good many ordinary people who have had a remarkable gift for helping others to find and recognize the grace of God that is within them. Most of them have been trained in the Ignatian spiritual tradition and have shared characteristics of being straightforward, accessible, astute, humorous and humane in their dealings with people. Since I began serving in that tradition myself I have met too many people who tell me that they don't know how to pray, or that they have always struggled with prayer, and feel depressed by spiritual books because they always seem to be talking about a realm of experience they've never had, or types of people they could never hope to be. But then they start to talk about what does happen when they try to get in touch with the God within, or reach out to a God who is always beyond their grasp, and I feel like taking off my shoes, because I know for sure that I am standing on the holy ground of their lives.

The seventeenth-century French playwright Molière wrote a play called *The Bourgeois Gentleman* in which Monsieur Jourdain, a middle-class cloth merchant with social pretensions to noble status, hires a tutor to educate him in the art of 'speaking proper'. At one point in a lesson on the difference between prose and poetry, his tutor reveals to him that he has been speaking prose all his life. Jourdain is delighted and astounded: 'My faith! For more than forty years I have been speaking prose without knowing anything about it!'

1

Many people could say the same about prayer. They've been doing it for years, but are so convinced that prayer is some mystical and esoteric art, beyond their own stumblings, that they have convinced themselves that their relationship with God is inadequate. Of course at one level it is – when finite creatures try to communicate with the infinite our reach truly does exceed our grasp, as Robert Browning reminds us. There is always going to be a limit to what we can achieve – but that is the point of heaven. Much of prayer is like much of the bread and butter of human relationships. It is hard slog and can involve much boring routine with not a lot of feedback. I sometimes tell those I accompany that one of the most spiritually honest hymns I would choose is the soldiers' chant, 'We're here because we're here because we're here because we're here.' In some desperation I've found myself humming it during prayer in my time. The most important thing is for us to be here – simply to turn up. We may find ourselves doing nothing but fidgeting for the time that we had set aside to pray in the hope of some kind of blazing divine revelation, though most of us would probably just settle for a sense that God is at home and open to receiving visitors. I remind people that Teresa of Avila, one of the greatest mystics of all time, shook the sand in her hourglass because she was so maddened with impatience and boredom during a prayer time where nothing seemed to be happening. But underneath it all, beyond all words and thoughts, the Spirit of God is at work (Rom. 8.26). Jesus himself reassures us that a prayer in which we experience and express nothing but our own poverty is more effective and gives God greater praise than one in which we bask in our own spiritual worthiness (Luke 18.9–14).

But there are also mountain-top moments of connection and ways in which, by God's grace, we can be in touch with our capacity to know and feel the presence of God in all things, and Ignatius was a rare and gifted teacher in helping people discover how to do this. God's desire to break through and surprise us is without limit, and we have a built-in ability to respond, pitiful though it may seem to us. Acceptance of our poverty and realization that this is the very gift God is seeking from us can be the beginning of a powerful life of faith and loving relationship with God made visible in Jesus.

The twentieth-century American Trappist monk Thomas Merton was, by his own account, a very unlikely contemplative, who nevertheless became one of the foremost teachers of prayer and the spiritual life of his time. In a wonderfully encouraging passage he tells us about learning how to pray:

> In prayer we discover what we already have. You start from where you are and you deepen what you already have, and you realize you are already there. We already have everything but we don't know it and don't experience it. Everything has been given to us in Christ. All we need is to experience what we already possess.[2]

Praying the Ignatian way

As a way of engaging with Lent, an introduction to Ignatian spirituality seems a good notion full of potential for individuals as well as for groups. Our word 'Easter' comes from the Anglo-Saxon word for spring. Ignatius' Spiritual Exercises and their approach to fostering a deep and lasting personal relationship of intimacy with God includes an element of spring-cleaning. There is a certain sweeping down of cobwebs in the form of old, tired images of God and ourselves that no longer serve us well. There is an invitation to a more flexible approach to prayer, exploring and experimenting with ways that may bring the word of God to new life. The text of the Exercises is rather dull in and of itself and has little to recommend it as 'spiritual reading'. It's rather like reading a car manual in the hope that it will teach you how to drive. Ignatius wrote it principally for those accompanying others in their spiritual life, and it is thus somewhat technical. But it contains profound insights into how we can use our various human attributes to pay attention to God. It is extraordinarily modern in its understanding of human psychology and breathtakingly free in its approach to prayer. At the beginning of the text Ignatius describes his spiritual exercises as 'all the formal ways we have of making contact with God, such as meditation, contemplation, vocal prayer, devotions, examination of conscience and so on'.

He remarks:

> Physical exercises are good for tuning up muscles, improving circulation and breathing, and in general for the overall good health of the body. So too what we call spiritual exercises are good for increasing openness to the movement of the Holy Spirit, for helping to bring to light the darkness of sinfulness and sinful tendencies within ourselves, and for strengthening and supporting us in the effort to respond ever more faithfully to the love of God.[3]

There are no hard and fast rules here regarding what personal prayer is. It is 'every way'. For some people this involves reading Scripture or some other text according to the traditions of meditation like *lectio divina*. For others it will be about silent stillness before the altar, or an icon or some other focal point that lifts the whole self to the contemplation of God. Others find that they need to give themselves permission to draw or journal, to look at a photograph, or go on a walk or look out to sea. 'But that isn't prayer!' they protest. It can be, if such an exercise opens their heart and will, their mind and imagination, their bodily senses and deepest desires to God.

The Spiritual Exercises contain a further invitation and challenge to look at our attachments, the patterns of thought and behaviour that have become embedded within us, and to take an honest inventory of them. Where they hold us back, we are invited to let them go. Where new patterns beckon us forward, we are invited to have the humility, courage and generosity to overcome fear, complacency or whatever else has prevented us from giving them a try. The Exercises are an invitation to daily conversion to the call of Jesus as friend, brother, lover and captain of our souls, leading to nothing less than the transformation of our lives. For some it may involve a life choice to serve the reign of God in whatever capacity they are called to. For others it will be a call not to a what but to a how, involving changing the way they have habitually been themselves. Either way it means engaging with all our gifts and personality in loving and serving God, choosing the life more abundant that Jesus promises us, acknowledging the gifts that our Creator has given us and using them, by the power of the Spirit, for the transformation of the material world within which we find ourselves. This is not a bad plan of action for a thorough bout of spring cleaning.

The Ignatian spiritual tradition is not a specialist '-ism'. Had Ignatius himself heard the term 'Ignatian spirituality' I suspect he would have been both baffled and embarrassed. First of all, he knew that he had taken much of what became his *Spiritual Exercises* from earlier medieval texts, especially the *Life of Christ* by Ludolph of Saxony. In both Ignatius' text and Ludolph's we find a method of contemplating the Scriptures that uses the heart and the imagination, taught and practised by some of the greatest spiritual figures of the Christian Church, going back in a line from Bernard to Anselm to Augustine, with many more in between. As such, Ignatius did not think of this way of praying as his own invention. Instead he built on a fairly simple tradition of using our day-to-day human faculties of thinking and feeling as a means of helping people to read and internalize the words and events of Scripture and make them their own. His genius lay in finding a way to use this in a dynamic process of getting to know and understand ourselves better, seeing ourselves with God's merciful eyes, in order to recognize where we are bound by habits of thinking and behaving that trap us in damaging ways and prevent us from living the fullness of life which Christ promises us and for which we were created.

Setting out

This book is therefore not for people seeking complicated and 'advanced' methods of gaining expertise in the art of contemplation and mystical prayer. It's a book whose aim is to offer reassurance and confidence. Human beings are wired for God. It's in our DNA to be able to reach out or deep within and find the God who connects with us at so many levels of our human existence. For us it's a matter of discovering what is often buried in layers of distraction or beliefs that contradict our experience, like thinking that only holy people really know how to pray, so what we are doing can't really be prayer, or that prayer is something so 'other-worldly' that it can't have anything to do with day-to-day living in material bodies and concrete contexts.

This is a book for any time, but my own experience and that of many whom I have accompanied tells me that a boundaried period of time is often best when undertaking a focused and concentrated learning process. In so far as the book is intended to help people learn what, at their deepest level, they already know, a time like Lent is as good a time as any to get going, one step at a time. The Spanish poet Antonio Machado wrote:

> Traveller, your footsteps are the path, and nothing more.
> Traveller, there is no path, you make the path by walking.[4]

The best way to get going is to get going, on a road for which there is no map, but which unfolds before our feet if we have the courage to walk. One version of the gradual psalms, which Jesus and his family and friends would have recited on their pilgrimages to Jerusalem, says, 'Happy are those whose strength is in you, in whose heart are the highways to Zion' (Ps. 84.5). The pilgrim way each of us is called to walk every day is the path of conversion. Someone asked me recently, 'So when did you become a Christian?' to which I replied, 'Today, I hope.' The book of Lamentations tells us, 'the steadfast love of the LORD never ceases, his mercies never come to an end; they are new every morning' (Lam. 3.22–23). In that sense our opportunities to start afresh are also new every day, irrespective of what has gone before. In the memoir of his life that a reluctant Ignatius was persuaded to dictate to a companion, he never named himself but called himself 'the pilgrim'. I hope this book will be a helpful introduction to Ignatius and others who followed in his way as companions on your pilgrim road. Use it if it helps, set it aside if it doesn't, but above all trust in the God who would not have encouraged you to open its pages if there was not potentially something in it that would guide your steps. Each chapter comes with some questions to reflect on either alone or with others. If they don't help, but other questions emerge instead, follow your instincts and stay with those. When I was a schoolteacher my pupils would often put up a hand and say, 'I know this is a stupid question, but . . .' I would tell them that there is no such thing as a stupid question. The only stupid thing is not to ask questions.

Questions for reflection or discussion

1 What do you think prayer is? Have you found a way to pray that works for you, or have you read anything here that encourages you to branch out into new ways?
2 Can you remember ever having a sense of God's presence in your life? What was that like, and what did it lead to?
3 There are numerous Ignatian websites that offer help in learning to pray. Can you find any particular one that has helped you? You might like to try

<www.pray-as-you-go.org/home/>

2

How it all works

As Ignatius discovered more about how God was at work in his life, he kept a notebook of what helped him to come closer to God and understand God's ways. He came to realize that what had helped him could be of help to others too. The notes would in time become his *Spiritual Exercises*. Organized into four so-called 'Weeks', they don't correspond to seven-day blocks of time but to different stages in the process towards spiritual freedom and renewal, and wholehearted commitment to serving God as a friend and disciple of Jesus.

These Exercises can be done in a variety of ways, depending on people's circumstances and capacity. The most 'hardcore', in many minds, involves going to a retreat house for just over a month and making them in silence, withdrawn from the normal framework of our lives, and accompanied by a trained guide. Some temperaments need this kind of full immersion, but others find the 'Retreat in daily life' more suited to them, whereby they follow the path of the Exercises over a longer period of time while still in their home setting. They commit time and energy to the enterprise but remain within their normal context. In between these two ways lies a huge variety of shortened forms of retreat or focused spiritual engagement, which can be from two or three days to a week. Ignatius did not intend everyone to make the full Exercises and they are not suitable for everyone.

The First Week of the Exercises begins with seeing our life and our purpose in the world within the perspective of God's unending and unquenchable love for us. We exist in relationship with everything that God has created, since its purpose is to help us to become our truest, God-given self. We are faced with the awareness that the way we choose to interact with creation, our relationship with ourselves and others, may help but also may hinder our loving response to God. God's greatest gift to us is freedom, so we are invited to acknowledge whatever gets in the way of our freedom and ask God to liberate us from our self-chosen slavery. From this position of honest and radical encounter with our un-freedoms we come to know ourselves as loved and forgiven sinners and we hear the invitation of Jesus to follow him as his friends.

The Second Week is a school in discipleship in which we trace the pattern of God's choices. It starts with the loving God-in-relationship that is the Trinity, opting for our sake to be born into our world in human flesh in the person of Jesus. We follow him through childhood and growth into adulthood. We become familiar with him as a person known by experience: 'what we have heard, what we have seen with our eyes, what we have looked at and touched with our hands' (1 John 1.1). By becoming his intimate companions, witnessing and sharing in his healing and teaching, we come to know what Ignatius calls Jesus' 'way of proceeding'. We learn to see the world and react to it the Jesus way and are brought face to face with a number of opportunities to 'see him more clearly, love him more dearly and follow him more nearly'.[1]

The Third and Fourth Weeks are inseparable, since the Passion of Jesus cannot be understood without his resurrection and vice versa. They are a school of the heart, in which we follow Jesus on the road to Calvary, meditating on his words and actions in the weeks leading up to his Passion and seeing how all of it is the ultimate expression of God's love for us in the Word made suffering flesh. The Fourth Week leads us to meditate on Jesus' risen life with his disciples and learn the difference his rising makes to the whole of human history and to the universe itself. With the disciples we walk with the risen Christ and accept his summons to go and announce the good news to all nations, loving and serving him in the circumstances of our concrete lives in the world.

The Exercises act as a pattern for living and praying a dynamic inner process, a rhythm of attraction and response in which we can go ever deeper into the truth of ourselves-in-God and God-at-work-in-us. This dynamic is paralleled in the rhythm of the Church's year, so that as the year and its liturgical cycle goes round, we are gently renewing our encounter with Jesus the second person of the Trinity, born into our world, living his hidden life of utter ordinariness, calling us to his side as he embarks on his mission and asking us to witness to his death and resurrection in order to live in his Spirit as

words made flesh ourselves, wherever and however we are invited to
do so.

When we discuss the Weeks of the Exercises, therefore, we are
talking at one level about specific moments in the text that refer to
a particular point within that dynamic rhythm in a retreat. But we
are also talking about any similar point in our life's journey, which is
often mapped out like a repeating spiral, with steps forward and back.
We may find ourselves in First Week mode, learning to see ourselves
with God's merciful eyes, learning to know ourselves as sinners, but
loved and forgiven, created by God for a definite purpose.

In Second Week mode we find ourselves receiving a call to
conversion and close friendship with Jesus, but there will be calls
within that call. Many people say that the reason they got married, or
went into ministry or made some other life commitment, is not the
same as the reason why they have stayed within that commitment. We
change as we age and as our vocation unfolds. The most important
vocation for any Christian is that of baptism, to become part of the
body of Christ, and it is a natural aspect of bodies that they grow,
change and mature. We have life rhythms that correspond to times
of self-exploration and fresh encounter with Jesus, times of close
companionship where in the light of his teaching and friendship we
take stock of what we are doing with our gifts, and feel the invitation
to make a commitment to something or someone in a bond of love.
Such commitments ask us to put others first and to empty ourselves
of egotistical compulsions. This can be demanding and challenging,
but the love of Christ and of others in Christ urges us on.

In Third Week mode we experience estrangement and loss; we
may face the death of those we love, or suffering in ourselves and
others. Our doubts and inescapable darkness come to the surface as
we confront the radical poverty within ourselves. That same fragility
is made manifest in Jesus, who empties himself of all power for our
sake, and in doing so overcomes all the darkness and dominance that
exists within the world. This is the moment of his greatest humiliation and greatest victory, and now the invitation is to share in this
victory by staying with him in his suffering. Instead of instinctively
wanting to escape, all we want is 'to know Christ and the power of his
resurrection and the sharing of his sufferings by becoming like him
in his death' (Phil. 3.10). That desire to know Christ crucified and
risen changes our perspective on the world for ever, and enables us to

see everything as resonating with his risen glory as well as reflecting his sufferings. We become truly able to find God in all things so that nothing separates us from that sense of being in what Julian of Norwich describes as our 'homeliest home'.

Tools of the trade

Prayer is a conscious and deliberate choice to enter into relationship with God, who finds many different ways of initiating the relationship. Ignatius teaches two primary ways of praying within the Exercises: meditation and contemplation. We are encouraged to use our mind and its capacities of reflecting, pondering and thinking about words and ideas that lead us more deeply into the meaning of Scripture. We are also invited to use our feelings, getting in touch with deep desires through imaginative immersion in a Gospel scene and using our bodily senses to draw us more instinctively and profoundly into direct, transforming encounters with God. This is not Bible study or the consideration of proof texts, but an intimate meeting with Jesus or a personal assimilation of the words of our Creator God. When we read history books about great figures like Napoleon or Marie Curie we can get a vivid sense of the person, but they are figures from the past, not alive to us in a way that changes us, as we change when we have face-to-face encounters with living people. In this way of prayer, Jesus is not a beloved figure from an inaccessible past but a living person whom we can encounter face to face in a way that brings about change in us.

Whatever way we can engage our minds, hearts and body in prayer and personal conversation with Jesus is prayer. We may have grown stale in a one-size-fits-all approach that has not grown with us. We may have become discouraged, needing to learn to become more disciplined or to loosen up in our relationship with God. Prayer, in this sense, is very much a matter of 'horses for courses'. We are encouraged to become brave and humble enough, in the words of the Benedictine monk Dom John Chapman, to pray as we can, not as we can't; by doing so, we may find that we can do more than we think. The Exercises suggest certain preliminaries before we engage with a Scripture passage. Some of it can seem rather courtly and elaborate, so we are tempted to write it off as Ignatius in full medieval courtier mode. But if we were preparing for a personal conversation with someone important to us we wouldn't rush into it straight off the street, our minds and bodies elsewhere. So Ignatius tells us to take our bodily posture and mental state seriously, in a way that helps us to be fully present and focused. This includes being mindful of whatever gift and grace we are moved to ask for. The asking isn't about the possibility that we might forget what we are desiring unless we mention it, but because such desires are seen to be a gift in themselves, and naming the desire prepares us to receive the gift for which we are asking.

Ignatius urges us to develop a sense of awe and reverence. This isn't just anyone we are coming before – it is the unknowable, unimaginable God beyond all our thoughts and words and imagining. The practice of reverence grows that sense of awe within us. But he also urges us to develop a sense of simplicity and affectionate confidence: picking up and cuddling the baby in the manger, thrilling with the joy and amazement of seeing the blind restored to sight, weeping as we see Jesus mocked and humiliated by brutal soldiers without a shred of mercy. This is intended to foster a real and heartfelt relationship with him within prayer.

Imaginative contemplation entails choosing a Gospel passage, for example a healing or an encounter between Jesus and an individual, and entering into the events and dynamics of the scene, perhaps as an onlooker, perhaps as one or other participant within the scene. All our senses are brought to bear in being as fully present as possible to the scene and to Jesus as he acts and speaks within it. Through our feelings and responses the scene becomes a living, personal encounter between ourselves and Jesus, in which we can speak, ask and love directly. Discernment is a key concept in the Ignatian tradition of prayer and we find it taught throughout the Exercises. Ignatius encourages us to take note of the directions in which our thoughts and feelings travel, noting the interior movements of our hearts, and following where they are leading us. We may be facing specific choices or simply trying to build discernment into our normal way of living more consciously and reflectively, being more 'switched on' to God in our everyday life. Either way, it can help us to make good choices and decisions in things great and small.

Above all, Ignatian spirituality is a very practical approach to the things of God. Ignatius believed that we are all called to co-operate with the Spirit at work in the world in order to transform it into what

God intends for it. There are no 'no-go' areas in creation because everything belongs to God. Therefore we are invited to develop a capacity to 'find God in all things' and to see the whole of life as a collaboration with our Creator. There is the properly secular sphere, in terms of what is not the specifically religious or ecclesial sphere, but while our call to sanctity is as people of faith, it is equally as people involved in family, business, study, agricultural or industrial labour, the arts or science or technology, people with particular histories, opportunities, illnesses, hopes and fears. We learn to integrate every part of our life: the spiritual, the financial, the social and the sexual, and live it to the full in Christ.

The monastic vocation is one specific call for particular people, not for everyone. Ignatius invites us to become 'contemplatives in action', living, speaking, thinking and acting contemplatively, even in the most banal of everyday acts. Every human faculty is enlivened by our intimate personal relationship with Jesus and is offered for his praise and service. Above all, Ignatius helps us to get in touch with our deepest desires, for this is where he believes that God is revealed at our very core. At Caesarea Philippi Jesus asked his disciples, 'Who do you say that I am?' (Matt. 16.13–20). The key question for us to ask Jesus in our own turn is, 'Who do you say that *I* am?' Ignatius teaches us how to hear and understand the answer, for it is in the light of that answer that we truly learn to know ourselves.

The examined life

Plato's *Apology* quotes Socrates as saying that the unexamined life is not worth living. Ignatius considered what he called the Examen as the most important of prayers, so important that he tells his fellow Jesuits that if, by force of circumstances, they are deprived of all other forms of prayer, or have to give one or other of them up, this is the one they must hold on to. It used to be called the Examination of Conscience, but this tends to have overtones of a self-denigrating and punitive list of one's latest mistakes – 'Oh God, where did I go wrong today?' A wise spiritual guide in the Ignatian tradition, American Jesuit George Aschenbrenner, wrote a famous article in the 1970s which took a different view, from which people began to speak about an Examination or Examen (from the Spanish term) of Consciousness, or Prayer of Awareness.[2] It did a huge amount to rehabilitate and popularize the Examen, but some more recent commentators have worried that this encouraged people to a type of prayer that leads to narcissistic introspection – 'It's all about Me.' Ignatius' aim was neither of these extremes. With the Examen he helps us to live reflectively and be conscious of where the details of our daily life are drawing us to or away from God. It's above all a prayer that leads to a spiritual awareness and sensitivity to God's presence or absence that can help us rebalance our lives in the light of the gospel.

There are several steps in the Examen. The first is to become aware of God's presence and ask for the gift to see the day with God's merciful eyes and understanding. Seeing our day from God's point of view may give us a very different perspective on it. Some things that seem of huge importance to us may be cut down to size, while others we gloss over or think trivial may assume their correct proportions. Ignatius constantly reiterates the importance of gratitude as the bedrock of our relationship with God, so he invites us here to review our day with gratitude. That may only mean saying 'Thank God I survived it', if the day has been hard, but we will develop the capacity to recognize the gifts within the day: a conversation or a thoughtful gesture from a stranger, friend or colleague, a meal, a breakthrough at work or in a relationship, a sudden awareness of beauty, the small pleasures and treasures of life. The details may be small but God is to be found within them, thanked and praised.

As we focus on events, we also focus on how they made us feel. Ignatius was himself a man of strong emotions, and learned to pay attention to them as a way of intuiting God's presence. What has provoked joy and confidence, or sadness and discouragement? We will inevitably find parts of our day that cause us some concern or pain, as we see ourselves or others fall short of the gospel ideal, but these can be the stuff of prayer for us, asking for healing, acknowledging our poverty and our need of God, sharing our thoughts and feelings.

We ask the Holy Spirit to make clear to us what we can learn from this day, whether positive or negative. We pray for God's grace, and name whatever emerges as something or someone for which we want to pray, repent or thank God. Finally we seek the Spirit's guidance for whatever lies ahead, praying in hope and sincerity. Ignatius' God is someone with whom we can have an honest and no-holds-barred conversation. The Examen is a very conversational prayer and its aim is to strengthen our sense of intimacy with the God who shines a compassionate and encouraging light on our daily reactions and interactions.

Questions for reflection or discussion

1 'God's greatest gift to us is freedom': what do you understand by inner freedom?
2 Is there anything in your life that prevents you from feeling free to be your best self?
3 Have you ever tried the Examen? You can find help on the following websites:

   <www.ignatianspirituality.com/ignatian-prayer/the-examen>
   <www.ignatianspirituality.com/19076/examen-prayer-card>
   <www.youtube.com/watch?v=P6hZyRkpLWw>.

3

Two journeys of self-discovery

I have a great desire, a very great desire indeed, if I may say so, to see a true and intense love of God grow in you, my relatives and friends, so that you will bend all your efforts to the praise and service of God.

(Letter of Ignatius to his family)[1]

In the chapters to come we will follow the life and progress of Ignatius as well as stopping to reflect on what a given stage in his life tells us about prayer and the spiritual tradition he initiated, which very much springs from his own personal faith journey. We will also hear about one of the great women within the Ignatian tradition, Mary Ward, since her life and work also offer added insights and dimensions to this exploration.

Who is this Ignatius whose spiritual guidance has made such a difference to people seeking God? Iñigo Loyola (1491–1556) founded the Society of Jesus, the Roman Catholic religious order of men also known as the Jesuits. He features in many caricatures as the sinister figure behind the Counter-Reformation, the soldier saint known for his fanatically rigorous military discipline and the begetter of all the manipulative double-dealing that comes under the heading of 'Jesuitry'. In more historically accurate and nuanced accounts, he comes across as a man of passionate generosity, deep humility and warm feeling who called his fellow Jesuits 'friends in the Lord'. The name he gave himself was 'the pilgrim', and it was on his own experiences as someone whose spiritual journey took him to many unexpected places that he based the Spiritual Exercises that made him famous.

Since the latter part of the twentieth century, Ignatian spirituality has become something of an industry. Its popularity lies in a spiritual and psychological insight that is remarkably modern and extraordinarily adaptable. When one of his contemporaries was asked who these exercises were for, he replied, 'For Catholics,

15

Protestants and unbelievers', by which he meant for anyone who is sincerely seeking God, whatever their starting point. In an article entitled 'Why Ignatian Spirituality Hooks Protestants', the author Joyce Huggett explains her attraction to Ignatian spirituality because it is a Bible-based movement of God's Spirit reflecting a thirst for God that engages the imagination and feelings in a way that can lead to deep personal conversion and commitment to spreading the reign of God in the world.[2] People of every version of Christian belief, as well as those with no formal religious affiliation at all, have worked with adaptations of the Exercises. A class of mixed Christian, Muslim and Jewish students who were recently studying Ignatian spirituality at London University came to the conclusion that the first part or 'Week' of the Spiritual Exercises could readily be adapted to work effectively in their own communities. In recent years they have been used to good effect in schools, factories, high-security prisons and on housing estates, among the homeless and increasingly online.[3] They are not magic and they can be hard work, but they do offer anyone who engages with their process freely and sincerely an opportunity to open themselves up to a God who is willing to meet us where we are. The rest is up to God.

Ignatius was a man who made his fair share of mistakes, and was humble enough to admit and learn from them. Later in life he was reluctant to share the wisdom that came from his personal experience, but his Jesuit companions nagged him repeatedly to tell them how God had guided him from the time of his conversion onwards. A relentless Jesuit scribe who would not take no for an answer more or less followed him around the house, pen in hand, until Ignatius gave in and dictated his *Autobiography* not long before he died. This is one source for our knowledge of him, but Ignatius speaks to us through the genius of his *Spiritual Exercises*, through the *Constitutions*, the rule of life he wrote for his Jesuit companions, and through the many letters he dictated to a wide range of correspondents. He also continues to speak through the lives and writings of people who have followed in his spiritual path. One of the foremost of these is the Yorkshire woman Mary Ward (1585–1645) who was heavily influenced by Ignatian spirituality from childhood and spent her adult life trying to open up new opportunities for women to serve God on the Jesuit model, despite entrenched opposition within a church that could not accept her

vision. Like Ignatius himself, she was a great traveller both physically, as she tramped across Europe on foot, and spiritually, learning
the ways of God by trial and error. Much of her writing is lost to us,
but her letters and autobiographical fragments, including a series of
paintings known as the *Painted Life*, will find their way into these
pages, speaking with an honesty and directness that come from
her native soil and a loving cheerfulness that comes from a woman
who described herself as 'apt for friendship'. Quotations from these
sources will appear in the pages to follow, as also from sources that
are not strictly speaking within the Ignatian tradition, but that illus-
trate it in a particular way.

The courtier

Iñigo, who later called himself Ignatius, was born in 1491 in his family's
ancestral home in Loyola, which lies within a mountainous region of
the Spanish Basque country. The thirteenth and youngest child of his
parents, he was orphaned young and grew up in a household managed
by his brother Martín and his wife Magdalena. His was the increasingly confident Spain of the Catholic monarchs, Ferdinand and
Isabella, who were building a superpower on the basis of the Castilian
language and the Catholic faith, having banished Muslims and Jews
from Spain in 1492. The New World was opening up the possibility of undreamed-of adventures and riches, while, when Ignatius
was 22, the Pacific Ocean was discovered by European explorers.
Tectonic shifts in the political and social world were happening
with the break-up of medieval Christendom through the Protestant
Reformation in Europe and the continued threat to the Christian
West from the Muslim East.

At the age of 15, Ignatius was sent to seek his fortune in the household of the chief royal treasurer who was a member of the Spanish
court and a personal friend of the king and queen. For the next
ten years Ignatius would enjoy a life of luxury and excitement as a
minor courtier, learning all the arts of courtly behaviour, dreaming of
knightly exploits and of a beautiful and noble lady whom he loved from
afar. His vivid imagination and his dreams of fame and fortune were
nourished on a diet of the courtly romances and adventurous tales that
were popular during a period that came to be known as Spain's Golden
Age, which was famous for the genius of its writers and artists of every

kind. By his own account, Ignatius at this time was a vainglorious, hot-headed gambler and womanizer, an impetuous brawler intent on his own pleasure and social advancement. Not all his adventures were chivalrous, and his riotous behaviour during Mardi Gras in 1515 led to accusations of serious crimes and pursuit by a magistrate. Ignatius pleaded clerical privilege and fled to the protection of the Bishop of Pamplona. While he successfully found refuge through his claim to be a cleric, the magistrate argued with some reason that Ignatius was a layman, carrying weapons, dressing extravagantly and wearing his hair long in defiance of the rules governing clerical tonsure. Ignatius escaped further punishment, but his fortunes changed when his patron lost his place at court, and he moved to the service of the Viceroy of Navarre, which was a key strategic position in the struggle for supremacy between France and Spain.

The soldier

In 1521 French troops marched on Pamplona. Ignatius was a member of the small Spanish garrison left to guard the city. Heavily outnumbered and under direct attack from the French, Ignatius' companions saw that they had no chance of winning and decided to surrender while pleading for their lives. Ignatius would have none of it and, in a death-or-glory speech, persuaded the commander to make a last stand. This heroic, if highly risky, strategy came to an end for the would-be hero when his leg was shattered by a French cannonball. The fortress surrendered shortly afterwards and the wounded Ignatius was sent home in a litter.

He underwent agonizing treatment to mend his broken bones and the physicians despaired of him. To their surprise he survived, but his leg had set badly in a way that offended his vanity, so he persuaded the surgeons to remove a protruding section of bone and stretch his leg with weights to prevent a limp. This torture resulted in his having to spend months in bed, immured in the quiet of the house's upper storey. Bored by all the inactivity, Ignatius asked his sister-in-law for some of the chivalric tales to which he was addicted. Whether she really had none in the house, or she merely pounced on this opportunity to turn her wayward young brother-in-law's thoughts in more pious directions, Magdalena produced a *Life of Christ* by Ludolph of Saxony and a book on the *Lives of the Saints*.

The convalescent

Ludolph taught a way of entering through prayer into the presence of God using the senses and the imagination. This appealed to Ignatius, and he found himself beginning to muse no longer on daring exploits by knights in shining armour but on the deeds of saints like Francis and Dominic. His mind had long been occupied with making a name for himself at court but now he found himself thinking about taking up service in the court of Christ the King. Where he had been all in favour of mad heroics in displays of military prowess, he began to think of the heroism of the martyrs and those who dedicated themselves, body and soul, to following Christ. Ignatius was now 30 and his courtly career had come to an abrupt end. He still had leanings towards his previous dreams of chivalry and romantic love, but he began to observe that, while hours spent in fantasy inspired by chivalric tales were thrilling at the time, the delight he felt led nowhere solid and in the long run left him weary, dry and restless. In contrast, although his fantasies about the hardships of a life of saintly asceticism were a far remove from wild adventure and passionate love, he derived unexpected consolation from the thought of imitating the saints, and this consolation, peace and joy proved lasting. This simple observation would in time underpin Ignatius' teaching about consolation and desolation and the 'discernment of spirits'. By this he means a way of understanding the movements of feeling, inclination of the mind and will, and how we pattern our life choices on being drawn or repelled by such inclinations. For now, Ignatius simply alternated between the two types of fantasy and the feelings that they aroused, but little by little he began to take notice of the different directions in which they led, and to try to make sense of what was happening within him. His first observation was simply that some kinds of thoughts left him inspired or happy, while others left him dispirited and sad. In time he came to think in terms of good and bad spirits, spirits that lead to or away from God and the things of God. It is for this tradition of discernment of spirits that Ignatian spirituality became chiefly famous and spread everywhere that Ignatius and his companions in the Society of Jesus ministered.

Another story

One such place was seventeenth-century Yorkshire. If we fast-forward some 80 years to Osgodby, we will find 15-year-old Mary Ward living in her aunt's household around the year 1600. Born in 1585, she lived during the worst period of persecution against recusant Catholics who refused to attend the state church. Her family over several generations were recusants who suffered fines and imprisonment for their faith. Her maternal great-grandfather, Sir William Mallory, had stood for two days with drawn sword outside his parish church 'to defend that none should come in to abolish religion'.[4] Her grandmother, Ursula Wright, spent 15 years in prison for her faith, and her aunt, Grace Babthorpe, spent the first five years of her married life in prison. Three of Mary's uncles would be killed for their part in the Gunpowder Plot, so she was no stranger to a culture of resistance and combat in a religious cause.

Mary was one year old when the York butcher's wife, Margaret Clitherow, was publicly crushed to death for sheltering priests. Margaret belonged, as did Mary and the women of her family, to an extended network of Catholic women who took inspiration from the example of the English Catholic martyrs and the zeal of English priests trained abroad, who ministered in secret to the Catholic underground movement. From this inspiration came a passionate commitment to their faith. There were no monastic houses left in Britain since the suppression of the monasteries under Henry VIII, but many of these recusant families lived according to an almost monastic regime within their homes, and became familiar with the Ignatian Spiritual Exercises through the ministry of itinerant Jesuits. In the absence of established Catholic clergy or hierarchy, many Catholic women assumed positions of religious leadership at home or within prison, following a life of common prayer and religious instruction. Outside the prisons it was often less risky for Jesuits and other priests to seek the collaboration of women than of men, and a generation of women emerged who, at great risk to themselves, lived at the service of the Church while not being professed nuns. Mary came from such a family of women and would become one of the great pioneers of women's roles within the Church.

At the time, the only way to protect oneself and one's family from punitive fines and raids was to move from house to house so as not to be at home when trouble called. For this and for reasons of her health Mary had a much-disrupted childhood in terms of where she lived, but she grew up knowing herself loved and cherished by her family. As a small child, Mary had been taught to pray by her grandmother, but in her autobiographical writings she says that, though she sat where she had been placed in order to pray, she 'spent the time in sports'.[5] She was eager to please and was not beyond subterfuge in order to gain the approval of those she loved. She was also painfully shy and inclined to be anxious about her spiritual well-being, while suffering from having no accessible spiritual guide on hand, it being so dangerous for Catholic priests at the time to travel and minister to those in their care.

At some point she asked a priest, who happened to be staying with the household, for some spiritual guidance and he gave her a book entitled *Spiritual Combat* by Lorenzo Scupoli, printed in secret and first edited in 1598 by the Jesuit John Gerard, who would later become a friend and supporter of Mary's attempt to live the Jesuit life for women. Offering strategies for achieving spiritual perfection, it was a favourite text of St Francis de Sales. It used military metaphors, making it clear that in struggling with the devil, who is the enemy of all human attempts to love and serve God, one must 'fight or die'.

Mary's character and life experience differed hugely from those of the soldier of Catholic Spain, yet she seems to have picked up, through the Jesuits who ministered to her family, a similar approach to the spiritual life. Although a shy and anxious adolescent rather than a sword-wielding adventurer, Mary was drawn into an encounter with God and a call to a serious spiritual life through a book, which she considered, 'the best master and instructor that I have had in spiritual exercises for many years, and one perhaps of the greatest helps, which until now I have enjoyed in the way of perfection'.[6]

Scupoli's text encouraged her to practise particular virtues in the rooms to which they were attached, so that asceticism might combat gluttony in the dining room, modesty might combat vanity in front of a bedroom mirror, and so on. While at the outset this seemed a good way of growing in the virtues, Mary soon found herself tied up in knots as she moved from room to room in pursuit of her daily tasks, and was never sure which of the virtues to be attempting to practise at any given time. She also fretted about whether or not she was undertaking this spiritual combat with sufficient vigour and began to sink into a morass of anxiety and discouragement. She tells us:

> There occurred such a multitude of manners and ways of producing various acts of virtue, and this with such eagerness, that what at first was easy and pleasing became on a sudden difficult and wearisome, and with the additional scruple that I did not obey good inspirations, not doing all which were presented to my thoughts as good, (a thing impossible from there being so many and so different).

Being too diffident to bring herself to speak to anyone, she suffered these anxieties and setbacks alone, until

> God compassionated my simplicity, and in this anxiety gave me courage to reason in this manner with myself: these things are not of obligation but of devotion; and God is not pleased with certain acts made thus by constraint . . . therefore I will do these things with love and freedom, or leave them alone.[7]

Like Ignatius, Mary was torn between conflicting feelings. She learned to pay attention to the responses that were aroused by her reading and to the way in which they left her. Although the *Spiritual Combat* was an admittedly excellent spiritual text, her way of putting its teaching into practice was leaving her anxious and distraught and not ultimately drawing her closer to God. She found a way to recognize that God's way of dealing with us is characterized by love and freedom rather than by fear and coercion. She was doing the same discernment of spirits as Ignatius had done on his sick bed some 80 years before.

Lessons learned

From the stories of the convalescent in two minds and the adolescent tied up in knots we learn some important lessons in the spiritual life. Feelings matter. Where they come from and how we allow ourselves to be led by our affective responses matters. This isn't to say that we should canonize every feeling as the ultimate authority, but feelings and the thoughts and imaginings that go with them can be a helpful gauge in knowing whether we are being led closer to or further away from God. If something leads to an increase in genuine faith, hope or love that bears good fruit according to the Spirit, it is likely to be of God. If something, even though good in itself, drives us back into ourselves in a way that ultimately erodes faith, hope and love and bears fruit that illustrates this, then it is unlikely to be of God. This refers to our relationship with God's own self, but also includes our confidence that grace is truly at work within us, sinners though we are, our hope that we can live a life graced by God, and our ability to love the self with which God has gifted us. Ignatius began to notice the difference between the way in which he reacted to heroic fiction, which led his imagination to centre on himself, and the way in which he reacted to biographies of real people who had dedicated their lives to God. These led his imagination away from self-absorption to focusing on God and doing good for others. He followed the origin, the nature and the ultimate result of those feelings – the whole trajectory from start to finish – and in that he began to get a sense of whether God was within the whole process or whether he was following 'the serpent's tail'.[8]

Mary began to notice that even a good and effective guide in the spiritual life could become a hindrance rather than a help if followed slavishly in a way that led to scruples and anxiety rather than to inner freedom. She found the confidence and courage to judge that it was better to give up good practices that were clearly not achieving their purpose and to trust instead in God's mercy and compassion and the inner wisdom with which she had been graced, even as a very young girl. Neither Ignatius nor Mary was a mystical genius or a spiritual virtuoso at the time that these shifts in awareness occurred. They were ordinary people setting out on a pilgrimage with God that would take both of them miles from their origins. What was distinctive in both was the way they came to trust God-within-them enough to put their experiences and insights into practice.

We find numerous references to fear and freedom in the New Testament. Paul reminds the Romans, 'you did not receive a spirit of slavery to fall back into fear, but you have received a spirit of adoption. When we cry, "Abba! Father!" it is that very Spirit bearing witness with our spirit that we are children of God' (Rom. 8.15), while the first letter of John claims, 'There is no fear in love, but perfect love casts out fear; for fear has to do with punishment, and whoever fears has not reached perfection in love' (1 John 4.18). And the second letter to Timothy says, 'God did not give us a spirit of cowardice, but rather a spirit of power and of love and of self-discipline' (2 Tim. 1.7).

Prayer is not a performance-related activity and fearful anxiety does not help us to grow in maturity in any relationship, especially not our relationship with God. Ignatius fell into fear-filled scruples later on in his pilgrimage, but both he and Mary Ward came to know a God who casts out fear. Lent is a privileged time to reflect on the spirit of power and love that God gives to us in contrast to a spirit of fear or spiritual paralysis.

Questions for reflection or discussion

1 Go over the story of your own life so far, looking for patterns of closeness to or distance from the God whose desire is for you to flourish. What has helped you to grow, and what has diminished your growth in loving intimacy with God?

2 Can you see areas in your life where fear dominates? How might you grow in freedom and overcome fear?

3 Is there something you want to ask of God, some inner dream or longing as yet unfulfilled? What happens when you put that desire before God?

4

The pilgrim sets out

*There's no discouragement shall make him once relent
His first-avowed intent to be a pilgrim.*[1]

As the weary months of convalescence went by, the balance in
Ignatius' thoughts and feelings began to change. The fantasies of
chivalrous deeds in which he featured front-stage centre began to
fade, while thoughts and desires in which God was at the centre
began to grow stronger. His fundamental character traits of passion
and impetuous energy remained very much the same. When God's
grace gets to work in us we don't become someone else, we become
more fully ourselves. This means that the best energies in us continue
to operate, even if some of the characteristics we would prefer to
lose also remain. St Paul is a case in point. From the zealot who was
willing to kill because of Jesus, he became the disciple ready to die
for Jesus and the greatest apostle of all times. Yet, by all accounts, he
remained an awkward character, quarrelling with most of his fellow
disciples who were themselves great saints but also flawed human
beings. Grace builds on nature rather than overriding it.

Now, instead of being a knight, Ignatius longed to be a pilgrim
and go to the Holy Land to witness to Jesus. It was typical of him
to want to undertake the challenge of what was still in his day a
perilous journey. It was also something that he would later feed
into his Spiritual Exercises – the belief that physically engaging with
spiritual things through our bodily senses is an important part of
prayer. If feelings are important, then so are matter and our bodies.
Far from being abstract and disembodied, Ignatius' understanding
of prayer is thoroughly concrete. He wanted to see and touch, hear,
smell and taste all that was familiar to Jesus as the backdrop to his
life and teaching. Perhaps he also thought that, far away from the
context where he himself had grown to be such a vain and belligerent
young man, he might find a life of holiness. It is often tempting for

25

us to think that the grass will be greener somewhere else, and that taking ourselves away from a context where we haven't been the person we dream of being will make becoming that person easier. Ignatius would learn slowly to engage with his real and concrete self rather than with a version idealized through fantasy. He would learn to look at his weaknesses without defence or excuse, and in doing so to encounter the fullness of God's mercy and compassion.

In defiance of his family's ambitions for him, he set out with the secret aim of becoming a poor pilgrim. In his own words, dictated years later, he was still blind to the subtler ways of God and had yet to learn any discretion in spiritual matters. His head was still full of fiery imaginings as to the great deeds of penance and spiritual heroism he would do for God. He was full of passion and enthusiasm, at the heart of which lay a natural generosity of spirit. There remains a touching, if rather comical, naivety about Ignatius at this time in his approach to the things of God. As he rode on his mule towards the shrine of the Virgin of Montserrat he met a Moor with whom he had an argument on religious matters. The Moor continued on his journey but Ignatius was left struggling with the impulse to find and kill him for his unacceptable views. In the end, luckily for both parties, he decided to allow his mule to make the final choice, and the animal led Ignatius away from his murderous intent. Ignatius' temperament was not changed by his conversion, but became oriented towards the good and an instrument in God's hands.

Becoming ourselves, only more so

In his book *Thoughts in Solitude*, Thomas Merton, another great disciple of Christ with a challenging temperament, wrote:

> Temperament does not predestine one person to sanctity and another to reprobation. All temperaments can serve as the material for ruin or for salvation. We must learn to see that our temperament is a gift of God, a talent with which we must trade until He comes. It does not matter how poor or how difficult a temperament we may be endowed with. If we make good use of what we have, if we make it serve our good desires, we can do better than another who merely serves his temperament instead of making it serve him.

This could be a thumbnail sketch of Ignatius at this point, still very much driven by the particularities of his temperament, but learning bit by bit to orientate that temperament towards its Creator. Merton goes on to say, 'The things that we love tell us what we are.' He continues:

> The Cross does not sanctify us by destroying human feeling. Detachment is not insensibility. Too many ascetics fail to become great saints precisely because their rules and ascetic practices have merely deadened their humanity instead of setting it free to develop richly, in all its capacities, under the influence of grace.[2]

Ignatius' spiritual teaching is light years away from a set of rules that deaden our humanity. What it offers is an invitation to become increasingly free of everything that thwarts the full, rich development of our humanity, with all its capacities. As the 15-year-old Mary Ward discovered in her struggle for holiness, we learn to embrace what brings us closer to God in love and freedom rather than acting compulsively to crush or submit to the driving force of our temperament. *Spiritual Exercises* is written in numbered paragraphs or annotations. Their opening statement, called the 'Principle and Foundation', reads like a manifesto setting out Ignatius' understanding of the purpose of human life in relation to God and all of creation. This version, written in modern English, expresses the breadth of vision and freedom of spirit that lies at the heart of how Ignatius came to see the world:

> God who loves us creates us and wants to share life with us forever. Our love response takes shape in our praise and honor and service of the God of our life.
>
> All the things in this world are also created because of God's love and they become a context of gifts, presented to us so that we can know God more easily and make a return of love more readily.
>
> As a result, we show reverence for all the gifts of creation and collaborate with God in using them so that by being good stewards we develop as loving persons in our care of God's world and its development. But if we abuse any of these gifts of creation or, on the contrary, take them as the centre of our lives, we break our relationship with God and hinder our growth as loving persons.
>
> In everyday life, then, we must hold ourselves in balance before all created gifts insofar as we have a choice and are not bound by some responsibility. We should not fix our desires on health or sickness, wealth or poverty, success or failure, a long life or a short one. For everything has the potential of calling forth in us a more loving response to our life forever with God.

Our only desire and our one choice should be this: I want and I choose what better leads to God's deepening life in me.[3]

Saying yes

This is a dense vision of the spiritual life, which repays reflective exploration. From the outset we are invited to encounter a God who says yes to everything that is truly us and who in turn invites us to say yes to ourselves, to the world and to all the goodness of creation. There are distortions of religion that tend to say no to the material world, or at best a very guarded maybe. This includes the human body and the sense life and sexuality that go with it. From this perspective people talk of 'having a body', as if our body were something we could hang up in the wardrobe at the end of the day, or leave behind when it doesn't suit us. But we don't 'have' a body – we are a body, and it is in that body that we learn to live and know the power of God shining within our fragile humanity. How we are in our bodies and in our human reality matters. Ignatius tells us that it is God's intention in creating us that we should be in intimate relationship with our Creator and with all else that is created. St Augustine of Hippo wrote in his *Confessions*, 'You have made us for yourself, O God, and our hearts are restless until they rest in you.'[4] It is that restlessness that drove Ignatius to explore his feelings on reading about Jesus and the saints of old. That same restlessness drove Mary Ward to move from the idea of a punishing God to a God of compassion, freedom and mercy.

The medieval mystic Hildegard of Bingen wrote:

Do not mock anything God has created. All creation is simple, plain and good. And God is present throughout his creation. Why do you ever consider things beneath your notice? God's justice is to be found in every detail of what he has made. The human race alone is capable of injustice. Human beings alone are capable of disobeying God's laws, because they try to be wiser than God.[5]

The Ignatian vision of a good and God-given creation in which we have a place of our own from all eternity is echoed by the letter to the Ephesians:

Blessed be the God and Father of our Lord Jesus Christ, who has blessed us in Christ with every spiritual blessing in the heavenly places, just as he chose us in Christ before the foundation of the world to be holy and blameless before him in love. (Eph. 1.3–4)

The first step in a spiritual pilgrimage in the Ignatian tradition is to embrace that goodness in creation, within ourselves and within others.

Choosing life

On the Thursday after Ash Wednesday the lectionary reading from the Hebrew Scriptures sees Moses offering the Israelites a choice:

> See, I have set before you today life and prosperity, death and adversity. If you obey the commandments of the LORD your God that I am commanding you today, by loving the LORD your God, walking in his ways, and observing his commandments, decrees, and ordinances, then you shall live and become numerous, and the LORD your God will bless you in the land that you are entering to possess. But if your heart turns away and you do not hear, but are led astray to bow down to other gods and serve them, I declare to you today that you shall perish; you shall not live long in the land that you are crossing the Jordan to enter and possess. I call heaven and earth to witness against you today that I have set before you life and death, blessings and curses. Choose life so that you and your descendants may live, loving the LORD your God, obeying him, and holding fast to him; for that means life to you. (Deut. 30.15–20a)

The emphasis is on choosing life rather than death and the choice is ours. The destructive alternative to life that Moses warns against is not the revenge of a punitive God but the result of the patterns of compulsive behaviour that a choice of not-God can draw us into. Idolatry is not simply a matter of primitive people bowing to heathen deities. Idolatry is the state of mind we get into when we put anything other than God into where God properly belongs. Today's celebrity culture is full of secular idolatry: the worship of fame, money, the body beautiful, social success, 'image'. These can all become idolatries in their own right. Holding fast to God is a profound yes to all that brings us freedom and growth.

The philosopher Friedrich Nietzsche had entirely the opposite idea of what being a Christian is about. He saw the Christian conception of God as 'one of the most corrupt conceptions of the divine ever attained on earth . . . God degenerated into the contradiction of life, instead of being its transfiguration and eternal Yes! God as the declaration of war against life, against nature, against the will to live!' While a great admirer of Jesus himself, he saw the New Testament as a vile misrepresentation, distorting the message of Jesus into a 'hatred of spirit, of pride, courage, freedom, liberty of the spirit . . . the hatred of the senses, of joy in the senses, of joy itself'.[6] It may be that Nietzsche had simply never met the right kind of believer who could help him adjust his bilious view of Christianity, but it may also be that some of the responsibility for his views lay with believers who lived a repressive and distorted version of faith rather than one that led them to enjoy the freedom of the children of God.

The Ignatian 'Principle and Foundation' is all about finding that freedom. Ignatius is careful not to canonize any one path to God as an absolute. He doesn't preach a prosperity gospel in which riches are a sign of God's favour, but nor does he present money itself as irredeemably evil. Like the writer of the first letter to Timothy, he teaches that it is when a love for money becomes disordered that it is the root of all evils (1 Tim. 6.10). The same goes for length of life, health or success. It would be a strange human being who had a marked preference for having a short, unhealthy, poverty-stricken life of abject failure. But Ignatius' point is that prosperity and poverty can lead to a good life or to one fixated on self-indulgence and the ruthless ignoring of the sufferings and needs of others. Jesus' own parables of the rich man and Lazarus or the sheep and the goats in Matthew 25 bear this out. He points to a failure to see that he himself is encountered in our fellow human beings, so that, in so far as we ignore the needs of the poor and suffering, we ignore God's own self-revelation: 'Truly I tell you, just as you did not do it to one of the least of these, you did not do it to me' (Matt. 25.45).

The pursuit of happiness

Despite the huge increase in our wealth in the past 50 years in the developed world, research confirms that our levels of happiness have not increased and if anything have diminished slightly.[7] The same research suggests that richer countries do tend to be happier than poor ones, but that once people have a home, food and clothes, then extra money has little effective power to make us much happier.

Lent is a good time to think of the ways in which we live within our bodies and are conscious of the bodies and bodily needs of others. Every meal that we eat and garment that we wear, carpet that we walk on or computer that we depend on, has been through God knows how many anonymous hands before it arrives in front of us for our use and enjoyment. The circle of consumption easily cuts us off from a sense of connectedness, meaning and social accountability. This is the message of prophets like Amos, Hosea and Isaiah, whose words are proclaimed to us in the Scripture readings for Lent. They speak in God's name to a society that has forgotten how to feel and live in solidarity, making an idol of the market and a deity of the profit margin. Religion itself can become a commodity, its symbols cut off entirely from the context of faith and community from which they emerged. Footballers and gang members wear rosaries; St Christopher sits on the dashboards of dangerously speeding cars; Tibetan prayer wheels, mezuzahs, dream-catchers and the hand of Fatima become de-contextualized objects with which people vaguely surround themselves in the hope that they will bring a little of what they call 'good luck'.

Relationships with family and friends are far more crucial to happiness than 'stuff'. Having meaning in life – a belief in something greater than ourselves, and having life goals embedded in our long-term values – is what really contributes to human flourishing. The trouble is that even these goods and values that contribute to human flourishing cannot shield us from the deepest threats to our happiness: disappointment, loss, lack of meaning, the breakdown of relationships, sickness and death – all the causes and fruits of human fragility. Nor can they ever fulfil, in the ultimate sense, our deepest longings. One translation of the first of Jesus' Beatitudes is 'Blessed are those who know their need of God.' Knowing that need, as the convalescent Ignatius came to know it, is the first stage on the pilgrim road to wisdom and right relationship with our Creator and all creation.

Deep desires

Many of St Augustine's writings express a profound theology of desire. He might be called the patron saint of desire, given that he is credited with that honest prayer, 'Lord, give me chastity, but not yet.' In one of his sermons, Augustine writes:

The whole life of a good Christian is holy desire. What you desire you cannot see yet. But the desire gives you the capacity, so that when it does happen that you see, you may be fulfilled . . . This is our life, to be exercised by desire.[8]

Ignatius, like his fellow student at the University of Paris, John Calvin, received a thoroughly Augustinian theological education. Reflecting on the transformation of his own desires from the idolatry of fame, success and money to wholehearted commitment to the God who is source of all love and flourishing, he thought a great deal about desire and the role it plays in our spiritual lives. Augustine knew, as Ignatius came to know, that there is within each human person a God-shaped space that nothing but God can fill. According to Augustine, the desire for ultimate values hollows out a space within us into which the living God can enter, in order to live in intimacy with us. Our greatest dilemma is that we often don't know and cannot express what we really, really want. We fear to become needy, naked and poor. Anyone who has ever felt real hunger or thirst, or unsatisfied desire of any sort, knows how uncomfortable and vulnerable it can make us feel. We are more likely to agree with Nietzsche that it is best to be self-sufficient, secure, super-human. Who wants to be needy? Ignatius' answer is we do.

The prophet Isaiah speaks of our wasting money on things that cannot satisfy, while ignoring God's offer of free nourishment for the soul:

Ho, everyone who thirsts, come to the waters; and you that have no money, come, buy and eat! Come, buy wine and milk without money and without price. Why do you spend your money for that which is not bread, and your labour for that which does not satisfy? Listen carefully to me, and eat what is good, and delight yourselves in rich food. Incline your ear, and come to me, listen, so that you may live.
(Isa. 55.1–3a)

Through the prophet, God goes on to offer an invitation:

Seek the LORD while he may be found,
    call upon him while he is near;
let the wicked forsake their way,
    and the unrighteous their thoughts;
let them return to the LORD, that he may have mercy on them,
    and to our God, for he will abundantly pardon.
For my thoughts are not your thoughts,

32

nor are your ways my ways, says the LORD.
For as the heavens are higher than the earth,
    so are my ways higher than your ways
    and my thoughts than your thoughts.
                      (Isa. 55.6–9)

Ignatius learned slowly but surely to tell the difference between fake and true consolation. This is not a faith that is anti-desire. On the contrary, he believed that we don't desire enough. We are encouraged to pray 'to be exercised by desire'. Only when we become people whose deepest desires are stretched in all directions will we come to know the God who is the origin and goal of all those deep desires, and whose reward is an ever-greater desire. Desire in and of itself may or may not come from and lead to God. We may be diverted from the true Spirit of God by our own rooted egocentricity, by values inconsistent with the gospel, or by distorted images of God that diminish our capacity to grow. That is where discernment helps to explore the origin, course and goal of all our desires. But it is also possible that within our deepest longings the Spirit is leading us to God and to God's longing for us.

All Jesus' longing for us is encapsulated in his words to the Samaritan woman: 'If you knew the gift of God, and who it is that is saying to you, "Give me a drink", you would have asked him, and he would have given you living water' (John 4.10). Jesus was not afraid of desire. At the Last Supper he said, 'I have eagerly desired to eat this Passover with you' (Luke 22.15). From the cross he cried out his thirst for us. When the man who had everything came to ask him what more he could have, Jesus looked at him with love and longing, and said, 'There is still one thing lacking. Sell all that you own and distribute the money to the poor, and you will have treasure in heaven; then come, follow me.' And the rich young man went away sorrowful, unable to tear himself away from the good things in life that had become a trap (Luke 18.22).

Doing the same thing differently

Augustine, another rich young man full of desires that were not rooted in God, lamented after his conversion that he had left it late to love the beauty of God that is ever ancient and ever new. But it is never too late to seek the true happiness that can be found in a heart that dares to be exercised by desire:

Late have I loved You, beauty so old and so new: late have I loved You. And see, You were within and I was in the external world and sought You there, and in my unlovely state I plunged into those lovely created things which You made. You were with me, and I was not with You.

The lovely things kept me far from You, though if they did not have their existence in You, they had no existence at all. You called and cried out loud and shattered my deafness. You were radiant and resplendent, You put to flight my blindness.

You were fragrant, and I drew in my breath and now pant after You. I tasted You, and I feel but hunger and thirst for You. You touched me, and I am set on fire to attain the peace which is Yours.[9]

The Principle and Foundation highlights the balance that is crucial in the discernment of our desires. The word Ignatius uses is 'indifference', which can be ambiguous in English as that word carries connotations of 'I couldn't care less'. Nothing could be further from Ignatius' mind. It is not about not being bothered, but about not clinging to anything, even any good, as an absolute. Authentic desire for God is mediated to us in various ways through God's own word in Scripture, through the tradition of the Church, through our highest principles and values and through commitments that we already have. A weary mother of small children may long for the quiet of the cloister. A monk struggling with loneliness and the challenge of life in community may long for the warmth and intimacy of family life. A frustrated idealist may be fired with a desire to leave job and home and go to look after lepers on the other side of the globe, while ignoring the fact that there are people urgently needing attention at home. We face the task of discerning where our greatest good truly lies, and it may be a recommitment to doing or living the same thing in a different way. Indifference, in the Ignatian sense, implies committing ourselves to a lifelong conversation between God and our 'innermost self' that allows space for God's word to ring true within us at this particular juncture in our lives and for God's action to be felt.

British guitarist Julian Bream is a world class musician. Largely self-taught in the guitar and the lute, he found, midway through his stellar career, that badly mastered techniques were causing him increasing muscular pain and paralysis. Bream consulted a medical specialist who told him that 30 years of incorrect self-taught techniques were causing damage that would permanently affect him if he did not relearn the techniques properly. No one listening to Bream playing would have heard anything wrong at all in his sublime music, but he was feeling it in himself, so at the age of 39 he set himself the hugely difficult task of learning to do the same thing differently.[10] It can be the same for people in many walks of life, not only in terms of professional technique or competence, but in terms of how they approach relationships and in the many ways of being themselves. We may be putting on a wonderful performance that impresses and convinces others, but paying a high price, or putting others into the position of paying the price in terms of the damage we do to ourselves physically, psychically or spiritually in order to do so. For the majority of people the task of mid or later life is not to revolutionize our lives entirely, and go off to the other end of the earth to re-invent ourselves. In some ways it can be far more challenging to face the toxic ways in which we have learned to function, and to realize that God is calling us to be our truest selves in love and freedom by letting go of patterns of thought or behaviour that no longer serve us well. This is the truth and freedom to which Ignatius invites us through the truth and freedom he himself learned and embraced on the pilgrim road.

Questions for reflection or discussion

1 What does 'choosing life' mean for you?
2 St Augustine speaks of being 'exercised by desire'. What desires exercise you at this present time?
3 What do you understand from the story of Julian Bream? What might 'doing the same thing differently' look like in your life?

5

Who do you say I am?

Christy plays in ten thousand places,
Lovely in limbs, and lovely in eyes not his
To the Father through the features of men's faces.[1]

Ignatius the pilgrim arrived at the shrine of Montserrat and, like a true medieval knight, decided to make a vigil of arms in front of the famous Black Madonna. There were still traces of romantic extravagance in his approach, which, like the incident with the mule and the Moor, ended in tragicomic drama. Wanting to be totally anonymous and to rely entirely on God, he decided to swap his costly clothes with those of a poor beggar. It was a grand gesture, which threatened to rebound on him when the beggar was later accused of theft, until Ignatius gave assurances that he had willingly donated his clothing.

After his vigil he made a full confession of his life and set out for nearby Manresa, changing his outward status and even his name, from Iñigo to Ignatius. He would spend the next 11 months there in prayer and penance, begging for alms, and this experience would prove crucial for what was to follow. Rather like the hippies of the 1960s going out to 'find themselves' in India and Nepal, Ignatius allowed his hair and nails to grow. Excessive penances ruined his health, which he was later to regret, and this taught him, as an older man with responsibility for his enthusiastic younger followers, to moderate their passions and remind them that we serve God better with good rather than with broken health. He lived in the manner of the disciples sent out by Jesus, with nothing but what they had on their back, ministering to the sick and the poor who came to him for spiritual advice.

Fighting the good fight

At first, Ignatius found joy in this life given over entirely to God, but he began to feel discouraged at the thought of a lifetime of poverty and penance and then was overcome by the torment of scruples. He went over and over his past misdeeds, but no amount of repentance and confession seemed to help. Suicidal impulses followed and gathered to a crisis until God's grace came to his rescue: 'The Lord willed that he woke up, as if from sleep.'[2] Like Elijah in the cave, the encounter with God did not come in earthquake, wind or fire but in the calm that comes from letting go of control and allowing God to lead the process. Ignatius had still in some ways been seeing himself as a hero, albeit a spiritual one. He had to learn to hand over the initiative to God and abide God's way and God's time.

A similar, if rather less dramatic, incident took place in Mary Ward's life. She grew up against a backdrop of the execution and martyrdom of Catholics for their faith. Like the young Teresa of Avila, teenaged Mary dreamed of a martyr's crown. A painting in the *Painted Life* shows a gruesome depiction of priests being hung, drawn and quartered, and Mary embracing various grisly instruments of torture. As she grew older, her grip on life grew somewhat stronger. In her autobiographical writings she tells us that, aged 15, she found her desire for a spectacular death waning, so she turned to God in prayer, fearful that her fervour was failing. The Greek word for 'martyr' means witness, and God reassured her that her greatest witness in life would be to embrace the call that she received and to accept any future troubles that it entailed with serenity.[3] Mary grew to be remarkably willing to accept the terrible trials she faced in adult life, sending letters to her sisters while imprisoned by the Inquisition, saying, 'I write from my palace, not my prison, for truly so I find it.'[4]

We can fall victim to the momentum of our own enthusiasms, even in the spiritual life, and both our pilgrims had to learn to let go of self-focused fantasies and hand the initiative firmly over to God. They both also learned to have a greater respect for the 'everyday God', the God of little things and the ordinary aspects of our human living. This is what Ignatius refers to when he speaks of 'finding God in all things'.

'Blessed are the eyes that see what you see'

The Catholic tradition within Christianity sets great store by sacramental signs. One definition of a sacrament is 'a sign that makes real what it signifies'. Ordinary things like bread, wine, water, oil, healing words and touch and the love between two human beings become signs that God is truly present in our daily living. One difficulty can be that these signs become so exalted and 'special' in our eyes that we can fail to see the God who is not only to be found in the Scriptures or in the specific sacraments of the Church, but also throughout creation. One famous academic who was a pioneer in ecology went so far as to suggest that through a literalist interpretation of Scripture and a disregard for the material world, Christians were largely to blame for the ecological crisis.[5] While this view is easy to refute, it must be said that, in comparison to other groups, Christians were relative latecomers to the ecological party and this may be because some Christians were so heavenly minded that they were of no earthly use.

There is a long Christian tradition that emphasizes the link between ordinary, everyday experiences and the presence of God, intuited through faith. Jesus is Emmanuel, God-with-us, God in a human body and with a fully human nature. Paul reminds us that all who are in Christ become his body. This means that our own bodies become places within which God dwells. They can serve as ways of being open to and mediating 'God-with-us' to one another. The cosmos itself, and all that God creates, can be treasuries of God's presence. The traditional Indian greeting, *namaste*, means 'the God in me meets the God in you'. The greeting acknowledges the divine presence within one another, but Ignatius also encourages us to acknowledge it in all creation as a gift from God. The redemption won for us by Jesus plays out within the ordinary lives of ordinary people and within human society, despite all its complexities. Nietzsche remarked, 'I might believe in the Redeemer if his followers looked more redeemed.'[6] The secret for us lies in discerning the redeemer among an often unredeemed-looking humanity. The nineteenth-century Jesuit poet Gerard Manley Hopkins was fully immersed in Ignatian spirituality. In 'The Wreck of the Deutschland' he wrote, 'I greet Him the days I meet Him, and bless when I understand'.[7]

Learning to discern the still, small voice of God amid the noise of the world is a matter of paying attention to the multiple ways in which God's self-revelation takes place, in glory and grandeur but also in the banalities of every day. We bless when we understand, but we often don't notice, and so don't understand. We have the experience, as another poet says, but miss the meaning.[8] Ignatius and Mary Ward learned to wean their expectations of God's interventions away from the dramatic and spectacular towards the unseen and unsuspected because hidden within the ordinary.

Ignatius received one very vivid and direct illumination from God in a mystical experience by the River Cardoner, in which he understood the whole of his own life and the life of the universe as being in harmony with God. Later in life he would say that it was from this experience, which he described as the greatest gift given to him by God in all his life, that he 'began to see everything with new eyes'.[9] He began to see that 'The world is charged with the grandeur of God'.[10] Developing a capacity for wonder, a contemplative stance before all of creation becomes the way to allow this grandeur to fill up our senses. St Thomas Aquinas, contemplating Christ in the bread and wine of the Eucharist, speaks of the 'Godhead here in hiding', but God also lies hidden within concrete experiences that we don't generally label as 'divine' or 'mystical', but that are every bit as expressive of God's presence as any exalted moment on the mountain top.[11] Encounter with Christ can also take place in the most everyday of human encounters:

> Christ plays in ten thousand places,
> Lovely in limbs, and lovely in eyes not his
> To the Father through the features of men's faces.[12]

Hopkins, who wrote those words, again reveals a profound understanding of the Ignatian perspective on creation and its implications for human relationships. Developing a sacramental vision of reality means finding in ordinary life signs that make real what they signify: that is, the presence of God. The signs may not be very visible, so this generally requires an adjustment to our perspective. From his prison, John the Baptist sends Jesus a message that reveals an unusual vulnerability in the firebrand prophet: he is overcome by doubts because the longed-for Messiah doesn't look or act according to the set picture John had in mind: 'Are you the one who is to come, or are we to wait for another?' (Matt. 11.3). Jesus tells him to look at the signs and believe in what he sees.

'This is my body'

Jesus claims a privileged presence within the bodies of the least of his sisters and brothers. We are challenged to find him there, but we are unlikely to be able to do so unless we have also found him lovely in our own limbs and eyes first. Ignatius learned the humility that starts from a place of self-acceptance rather than destructive self-denial. In Mary Ward's *Painted Life* we find another image that gives us a vivid illustration of this shift in perspective. In 1606 Mary was living in London, near St Clement Danes in the Strand. By this time she had had two failed attempts at living the life of a cloistered nun and had returned to London under something of a cloud, with her dowry spent and no idea what God was asking of her. She had tried to pray one morning, but found the formal attempt at meditation 'cold, and not to my satisfaction'. She then went about the banal but complicated task of dressing and arranging her hair. As she sat looking into the mirror she tells us that she was suddenly filled with a sense of the overwhelming grace and presence of God, and sat for two hours hearing nothing but the sound 'Glory, glory, glory' ringing in her ears.[13] It was St Irenaeus in the second century who wrote, 'The glory of God is a living human being; and the life of human beings consists in beholding God.'[14] This has often been translated, 'The glory of God is a human being fully alive.' At a period in Christian history much inclined to see the human person and especially the human body as steeped in sin, and when to be female was considered a serious disadvantage, Mary looked at her own image, saw what God had made and found it very good. It was from this experience that she overcame her childhood shyness and became the woman who, with courage and graciousness, paved the way to fullness of life for so many others.

Many contemporary writers on the Ignatian tradition have considered its contribution to a more inclusive spirituality of the body. In the Spiritual Exercises, Ignatius speaks of a delight and relish in the gifts and graces of God. He encourages us to pray with our senses and to keep them fully alive to the messages of God's presence within the created order. This includes our gendered bodies, our sexuality and our capacity for intimacy. Ignatius encouraged people to live life with passion, and part of each exercise is to ask God for what we desire. Our problem, in his view, is not that we have too many desires but that we have too few, or at least that we often live at a low level of desiring that isn't fully human. We may also have taken on board negative attitudes to the body or to gender that are not consistent with the freedom of the children of God. As a young woman, Mary Ward had internalized the cultural assumptions about women prevalent in her time, though she still baulked at them. In her search for her life's vocation, she tells us:

> I had no inclination to any Order in particular, only I was resolved within myself to take the most strict and secluded, thinking and often saying that as women did not know how to do good except to themselves (a penuriousness which I resented enough even then) I would do in earnest what I did.[15]

She came to realize that the historical categories open to women and the prevailing concepts of female holiness were too narrow. She knew that women were called to do great things, although she also believed that greatness lay in ordinariness or, as she put it, in doing ordinary things well. That insight of the ordinary nature of holiness, or the holy nature of the ordinary, cuts across all the dualistic thinking about grace and human nature that was common in her day and remains surprisingly common in ours.

Transparency, sincerity, self-acceptance, being true to ourselves – these are all ways of understanding what Mary is talking about here. Later, one of her major spiritual experiences was to see in a vision the person of Jesus enter into her heart to live there.[16] Echoing the Gospel of John, Jesus was to make his home in her, and invite her to make hers in him. She learned to see her gendered self as God saw her and to look at herself and others with eyes of compassion, acceptance and love.

The focus of the Ignatian vision of the self-in-God is not narcissistic self-absorption but the fundamental orientation of our vision towards God at work in a creation that includes our embodied selves, created in order to love and serve God in the world with all that we are. We don't see our lives in Christ in isolation from our cultural and historical context. Our thoughts about gender, class, race and orientation tend to come from the background of our origin and can dominate the way in which we construct our view of God and what is acceptable in God's eyes. This can become the root of judgements we make about others and about ourselves that are far from God's mercy. The mystery of human relationships is very much in the foreground of Christian controversy today. It is a vexed question, full of pain and confusion, to which there is no easy answer. But if the Spirit blows where it wills, and if the Spirit is present wherever a bond of true love is present in a way that is creative, self-giving, liberating and faithful, then we should at least be wary of confining that Spirit to categories of our own devising, however hallowed by tradition. Jesus' conversation with Nicodemus, the teacher in Israel, warns him of the limitations of his own categories, even those that serve to define and point to the very presence of God in human affairs (John 3.8–10).

God's merciful eyes

Lent is a time for soul-searching and for looking at ourselves honestly. The anonymous English author of *The Cloud of Unknowing* tells us, 'It is not what you are nor what you have been that God looks at with his merciful eyes, but what you desire to be.'[17]

Learning to look at ourselves and others with such merciful eyes lies at the heart of any major conversion and includes a positive understanding of the embodied human person. The starting point is trust that God's gaze is, in fact, merciful. In the early phase of an Ignatian retreat people are often encouraged to pray with Psalm 139. It speaks of a God whose gaze is inescapable, but also of the gratitude of discovering within that gaze the wonder of our being.

> O Lord, you search me and you know me,
> you know my resting and my rising,
> you discern my thoughts from afar.
> You mark when I walk or lie down;
> you know all my ways through and through.
> Before ever a word is on my tongue
> you know it, O Lord, through and through.
> Behind and before, you besiege me,
> your hand ever laid upon me.
> Too wonderful for me, this knowledge,
> too high, beyond my reach.
> O where can I go from your spirit,
> or where can I flee from your face?
> If I climb the heavens, you are there.
> If I lie in the grave, you are there.
> If I take the wings of the dawn
> or dwell at the sea's furthest end,
> even there your hand would lead me,
> your right hand would hold me fast.

If I say: 'Let the darkness hide me
and the light around me be night,'
even darkness is not dark to you,
the night shall be as bright as day,
and darkness the same as the light.
For it was you who formed my inmost being,
knit me together in my mother's womb.
I thank you who wonderfully made me;
how wonderful are your works,
which my soul knows well!
My frame was not hidden from you,
when I was being fashioned in secret
and moulded in the depths of the earth.
Your eyes saw me yet unformed;
and all my days are recorded in your book,
formed before one of them came into being.
To me how precious your thoughts, O God;
how great the sum of them!
If I count them, they are more than the sand;
at the end I am still at your side.
O God, that you would slay the wicked,
that men of blood would depart from me!
With deceit they rebel against you,
and set your designs at naught.
Do I not hate those who hate you,
abhor those who rise against you?
I hate them with a perfect hate,
and they are foes to me.
O search me, God, and know my heart.
O test me, and know my thoughts.
See my path is not wicked,
and lead me in the way everlasting.
               (Ps. 139, Revised Grail Psalter)[18]

Many people find the antagonistic verses towards the end of this psalm shocking, and some lectionary readings avoid them altogether. They are uncomfortably reminiscent of painful periods in human history where religiously fuelled violence has torn entire communities apart. Surely such sentiments of hatred and aggression can have no part in a spiritual tradition that is supposed to integrate the gospel commands to love self and neighbour? There is a counter-argument that says that praying this psalm in a way that connects with the reality of our lives needs to include getting in touch with all that is not of God there, whether it is internal or external. This involves the expression of our negative thoughts and feelings and an honest appraisal of aggressive emotions and attitudes that we ourselves hold or that have been held against us. It can also help to give robust voice to all that we want to reject that comes under the category of what Ignatius calls the 'enemy of human nature'. For those who have long repressed any feelings and memories that appear less than worthy, or who have deep wounds to overcome, this can prove a considerable challenge. God meets us within the real, so prayerful encounters with such a God require honesty from us rather than hiding behind pious subterfuge. Only then can the deepest recesses of our lives lie open to God's healing mercy.

Our bodies awakening

The Principle and Foundation says that all things in this world are created because of God's love and become a context of God's gifts. This includes our bodily selves, but a distorted and dualistic view of the human body and human sexuality fuelled by repressive versions of Christianity can prevent us from believing ourselves entirely loved by God. Equally we can be on the receiving end of other people's projections about sexuality, which can induce deep-set feelings of shame and unworthiness. If anything, our current 'liberated' Western culture has made this worse. Selfie generation is never far from a camera and from the relentless pressure exerted by the fashion and beauty industries and the media to look perfect. This is affecting young men as well as young women. Dating websites place photos of potential dates online, and people are encouraged to assess one another solely on standards of physical attractiveness. It is not that far from the slave markets of the ancient world.

Symeon the New Theologian (AD 949–1022) was a Byzantine Christian monk and poet. He became abbot of the Monastery of St Mammas, a reformer with a considerable reputation for sanctity who nevertheless fell into such conflict with church authorities that he was eventually sent into exile. His writings share his own mystical experiences of God as divine light and are included in the *Philokalia*, a collection of texts by early Christian mystics on contemplative prayer. His poem 'We Awaken in Christ's Body' offers a vision of the wounded human person made whole in the light of Christ's mercy. It speaks of the sense of oneness with Christ that we find threaded through the Ignatian Exercises and other sources within the tradition. It is the absolute antithesis of the cult of the body beautiful, and can be profoundly healing for those whose self-image has been damaged in any way.

> We awaken in Christ's body
> as Christ awakens our bodies,
> and my poor hand is Christ, He enters
> my foot, and is infinitely me.
>
> I move my hand, and wonderfully
> my hand becomes Christ, becomes all of Him
> (for God is indivisibly
> whole, seamless in His Godhood).
>
> I move my foot, and at once
> He appears like a flash of lightning.
> Do my words seem blasphemous? – Then
> open your heart to Him
> and let yourself receive the one
> who is opening to you so deeply.
>
> For if we genuinely love Him,
> we wake up inside Christ's body
> where all our body, all over,
> every most hidden part of it,
> is realized in joy as Him,
> and He makes us, utterly, real,
>
> and everything that is hurt, everything
> that seemed to us dark, harsh, shameful,
> maimed, ugly, irreparably
> damaged, is in Him transformed
> and recognized as whole, as lovely,
> and radiant in His light
> in every last part of our body.[19]

To pray with this passage is not to wallow in self-adulation. It is to find in Christ's body a way of accepting and embracing our own body and finding within it the temple of the Holy Spirit. This is the starting point of a whole new life in Christ.

Questions for reflection or discussion

1 What do you understand by the 'sacramental vision of reality' discussed in this chapter? What difference would having such a perspective make to your way of perceiving and responding to the world?

2 Ignatius and Mary Ward learned to let go even of their most cherished dreams and to hand over the initiative for their lives to God. What might be the challenges involved in doing this? What would be most challenging for you?

3 How does the section on prayer in and through the body and the senses strike you? How does it feel when you try to pray through your own body?

6

The Spiritual Exercises
Purpose and method

———◆———

Lord Jesus, think on me, and purge away my sin;
From earthborn passions set me free and make me pure within.
(Lenten hymn)[1]

In this chapter we look at how Ignatius' Spiritual Exercises transformed the lives of those who became his companions and how
they have the capacity to transform our lives. We consider how
the method within the Exercises differs for the pilgrim making the
spiritual journey and the person accompanying that pilgrim. Through
the person of Simon Peter we see how the path to discipleship often
follows a familiar pattern.

Ignatius left Manresa and set out for the Holy Land to fulfil his
dream of seeing the land of Christ's birth, life and death with his own
eyes and if possible staying there in order to be of some spiritual help
to those he encountered there. But the situation of Christians in those
parts was extremely precarious and in the end he was ordered by the
leader of the Franciscan friars who were guardians of the holy places
to return home. The Franciscan had jurisdiction in the name of the
Church over all pilgrims to Palestine, so Ignatius obeyed him and
set sail once more. His travels led him to Barcelona and eventually
to Paris, as he realized that he needed to study theology if he was to
fulfil effectively his new dream of helping souls. He did this by the
example of his own prayerfulness, his preaching and above all his
teaching of ways of praying that would enable people to encounter
Jesus alive and accessible in the Scriptures, just as he himself had
done. Slowly but surely he developed the Spiritual Exercises that
would become the most powerful instrument in the realization of
this call from God. Their aim was to free people from disordered
attachments so that, with a new-found inner freedom, they could

make space for Jesus to become the centre of their lives and freely choose to follow him in whatever way he invited.

This called initially for a readjustment of perspective and attitude towards the things of this world, seen now neither as an attractive lure nor as a dangerous temptation. All of God's creation was to be seen and experienced as good, but, according to the difference in temperaments and vocations, some would learn to serve God as disciples of Jesus by full immersion in the world, freed from the compulsions of acquisitiveness, pride and vanity, while others would respond to a call to leave all for Jesus' sake. Neither path was seen to be an absolute divine imperative, though the former courtier turned poor pilgrim would always see actual poverty as a particular sign of God's favour.

In Paris Ignatius met and began to gather a group of companions who together would found the Society of Jesus, who became known as the Jesuits. In the fifth annotation of the Exercises it says:

> The most important qualities in the person who enters into these exercises are openness, generosity and courage. As retreatants, our one hope and desire is that God will place us with his Son so that in all ways we seek only to respond to that love which first created us and now wraps us round with total care and concern.[2]

These qualities of openness, generosity and courage are called for today from anyone praying in this way. Facing the truth about ourselves, acknowledging where disordered attachments limit our inner freedom and determining to overcome them by God's grace all take honesty, courage and a willingness to be changed. The word 'attachment' suggests that this is something we actively desire and willingly cling on to, but that is not always the case. Sometimes we carry deep wounds from our early life or from some traumatic experience. We may have learned to hate and fear something about ourselves. We may have been belittled and judged by others, and have learned to belittle and judge ourselves in an endless 'chorus of disapproval' playing in our minds. So sometimes learning to let go of disordered attachments means coming to see wounds for what they are and finding the courage to accept healing and learn to be more merciful with ourselves. This is what we encounter in the First Week of the Ignatian Exercises. Having established as fully as possible, through the Principle and Foundation, that we are chosen and loved by God in a bond that God will never break, we are then brought face to face with woundedness and also with sin, both our own personal sins and the systemic sin that besets the world. We belong willingly or unwillingly to whole networks of relationship – social, economic and personal – which can be toxic and destructive even when we don't will this to be so. We cannot simply withdraw from all human interaction in order to avoid being part of unjust systems, so we inevitably become tainted and compromised through our participation in them. When we look at our own responsibility for wrongdoing, or at our collusion in it by willing or unwilling participation, it is not so as to feel crushed by guilt and self-loathing but so that we can find more deeply the love and forgiveness of our compassionate God.

The guide and the pilgrim

When Ignatius was at Manresa he felt keenly the lack of anyone to guide or accompany him, begging God to send him even a dog to follow. In the end he did find help through the companionship of an elderly woman who was known locally to be spiritually wise. Having a companion is not about handing over personal responsibility, or letting that person take over from the Holy Spirit, but about having someone to whom we can articulate what is happening in our pilgrim journey with God. Sometimes we don't know what we are feeling or thinking, deep down, until we hear ourselves explain it to someone else. Ignatius gives the person directing the retreatant various guidelines for dealing with possible responses to the process of making the Exercises.

In the world of Ignatian spirituality there are many discussions about the names to give the respective roles here. For some people the term 'spiritual director' is problematic on two counts. First, it seems to suggest that all that is talked about or dealt with here is in some ethereal spiritual realm that is far from the earthy realities of daily life. Second, the word 'director' suggests someone who is pushing or prodding in a particular direction, limiting the freedom of the person being directed. It highlights an imbalance of power in the relationship and threatens to get in the way of a direct relationship between God and the retreatant. Other images have been suggested. One is to think of the director as a midwife. Her job is to reassure and tell the woman giving birth when she needs to push and when she needs to hold back, but she cannot give birth to the baby herself, only the mother can do that. Another image is that of a gardener, whose job is to hoe the ground and water it when it is dry, but not to pull up the plants every few days to check if they are growing correctly. The best gardeners allow plants to grow in their own way and at their own rhythm. Another image is of the accompanist of a solo performer. This person's task is to keep the soloist in tune and in proper rhythm, and to offer a context that gives depth and harmony to what is being played, but not to drown out the actual performance. Some prefer to speak of the retreatant as the pilgrim and the director as the guide or companion. This last reference seems preferable as it reminds us that this is, in fact, a triangular relationship between God and both parties. Both are listening to and being guided by the Holy Spirit, who is the only true spiritual director.

Whatever name we choose, it is a good thing to have someone with whom it is possible to be honest and who can listen attentively for the rhythms of the Spirit, give feedback, reassure, challenge and above all walk with us as a fellow pilgrim. Ignatius has advice for the guide at given times called the Rules for the Discernment of Spirits (*Sp.Exx.* 313–336). These are not something Ignatius invented but are part of a very old Christian tradition going back to St Paul (1 Cor. 2.6—3.4; Gal. 5.16–26). They assume that we are able to detect the presence of the Holy Spirit at work in our lives and also the work of a contrary spirit.

The divided self

Eighteenth-century philosopher David Hume gave a pithy description of the very mixed bag that is the average human being: 'There is some benevolence, however small, infused into our bosom; some spark of friendship for humankind; some particle of the dove, kneaded into our frame, along with the elements of the wolf and serpent.'[3]

St Paul knew a great deal about the divided self, and in his letter to the Romans gives one of the most poignant insights ever written of what it feels like to engage in the struggle to overcome one's fragilities. It is a portrait with a familiar ring for many people who have repeatedly tried to overcome their weaknesses only to be defeated, despite their best intentions.

So I find it to be a law that when I want to do what is good, evil lies close at hand. For I delight in the law of God in my inmost self, but I see in my members another law at war with the law of my mind, making me captive to the law of sin that dwells in my members. Wretched man that I am! Who will rescue me from this body of death? Thanks be to God through Jesus Christ our Lord! (Rom. 7.21–25)

From his late medieval perspective Ignatius uses the language of spirits. Theological opinions today differ on the existence of Satan, demons and angels as objects of belief. A modern reader might find this problematic and use more psychoanalytical or social scientific language, but the experienced reality is the same, that of someone in the grip of toxic patterns of thinking and behaving and at the mercy of inner drives. Ignatius' rules speak of consolation in a person deeply oriented towards God acting unobtrusively and peacefully, like water slowly soaking into a sponge. Conversely, desolation to such a person works in the enervating way of a constant, noisy drip of water.[4] He also looks at the person caught up in a sinful and damaging life and how such a person is tempted to stay within it. Generally this will be through complacency and the pleasurable sense that there are still more delights out there to be tasted: just one more won't do any harm, it's only for today – I'll give it up tomorrow, everyone else is doing it, I deserve a bit of a treat. Sensual and emotional justifications for gratification beckon and there is no inner drive or incentive to change such a way of life. These, he says, are the tactics of the evil spirit. This is not just about 'living *la vida loca*' in terms of endless days of wine and roses. It can also be about the gratification of the lust for power, wealth, celebrity or whatever drives us in a direction far from the way of Jesus.

The tactics of the good spirit in such a case are to disturb the conscience of this person with uneasiness, remorse and a sense of shame. These are uncomfortable feelings, but they can lead to change and liberation. We realize, deep down, the price we and those around us are paying for our compulsions. We know that we can be better than this, and that is both a sorrow and the dawning of hope for a new direction in life. So in this case consolation and desolation can be, as it were, turned on their heads. What feels 'consoling' may be embedding us more deeply into addictive and ruinous patterns, whereas what is pulling us away from them can feel disturbing. We are not just talking about what makes us happy and what makes us sad here, but about what builds up the life of Christ within us and what drains it away. This is why the Examen is such an important prayer, since it looks not only at what is happening in the specific-ally 'spiritual' part of our lives but also at what is happening in the ordinary texture of our daily living.

It is not uncommon for a religious community to include someone who is thought to be a saint in external society but who is a demon in the domestic environment. This can happen in families as well. Some of us are good at wearing masks outside, but we take them off at home, where people's good opinion does not matter so much to us. The Examen looks at consolation or desolation as the letter to the Galatians does, in terms of the fruit of what lies within us. We may not be getting much out of being disciples of Christ in terms of felt rewards. Mary Ward intuited that oppression and persecution from within the Church was looming, as church authorities did their best to dismantle her life's work because they disapproved of women claiming a public space. She wrote to one of her sisters that she could foresee a 'long loneliness' coming her way, yet she held on in faith, hope and love. In the aftermath of the death of Mother Teresa of Calcutta, her biographers revealed that she had spent years spiritually in a 'dark night' with little or no conscious, felt satisfaction in her prayer life. Yet for both these women the fruits of their lives in God were goodness, mercy, love, joy, peace and patience. Mother Teresa started her religious life as a Mary Ward sister and knew the Ignatian tradition well. She would have known and been conscious of this 'dark consolation'.[5]

This is all distinct from the feelings connected with medical condi-tions like clinical depression. It would be important to distinguish these and to seek appropriate help, making use of the scientific gifts given by God to the medical profession for our help and healing. Spiritualizing such conditions is not generally helpful, though faith in a God who comes to our help even in the darkest times may well be part of a healing process.

In the reverse situation, when a person is living a good life and trying their best to follow the leading of the Holy Spirit, tempta-tions tend to come in the shape of disturbing and desolate thoughts: I'll never be any good at this; no one else is living like this and they all seem to be doing all right; everyone will think I'm an idiot; I won't be able to keep this up; maybe it's all an illusion anyway.

Both Ignatius and the young Mary Ward suffered the tortures of scrupulous anxiety, thinking themselves spiritual failures, far from God's forgiveness. Such thoughts can surprisingly attack very good people, who can see God's mercy for everyone else but are unable to shake off feelings of deep unworthiness in themselves. These disturbances are not the prod of an awakening conscience but the tricks of a spirit of fear and self-condemnation, a spirit that is, as Paul says to the Galatians, moving us away from the general direction of our will for right relationship with God. Ignatius tells us:

> The evil one attempts to rouse a false sadness for things which will be missed, to instigate an anxiety about persevering when we are so weak and to suggest innumerable roadblocks in walking the way of the Lord. And so the evil spirit tries discouragement and deception to deter us from growing in the Christ-life. (*Sp.Exx.* 315)

He describes desolation as weighing us down with a sense of heaviness, spiritual restlessness, lukewarmness, a turning away from prayer and God's service that leads to feeling alienated from God. If we think of it as a spiral, it is a turning inwards on ourselves in a spiral that is self-centred. Contrarily, he describes consolation as being on fire with the love of God and able to love all created things in relation to their Creator. He also talks of consoling tears, when perhaps we are moved by love or saddened by our failures, but always in a way that enables us to grow in knowledge of and confidence in the saving love and power of God as our loving Saviour. This is a turning outwards from ourselves to God and to others, even when we are conscious of our own needs. Finally, Ignatius names as consolation any increase in faith, hope and love, and anything that attracts us to God and leads us to peace.

Peter: a case study

'Go away from me, Lord, for I am a sinful man!' (Luke 5.8)

Many of the more traditional Lenten hymns lay emphasis on the shame and confusion of knowing ourselves to be sinners. Some people talk of Christianity as being harmfully and deliberately guilt-inducing, but the story of the sinful woman in Luke 7 tells us otherwise. Simon the Pharisee, in the glow of his self-righteousness, passes judgement both on the woman (who is no better than she should be) and on Jesus (who ought to know what kind of woman this is). Jesus says to him: 'I tell you, her sins, which were many, have been forgiven; hence she has shown great love. But the one to whom little is forgiven, loves little' (Luke 7.47). He makes a direct correlation between her awareness of her sins and her capacity to love, demonstrated extravagantly in her kissing and anointing of Jesus' feet after bathing them with her tears. If we want to become great lovers of God, he implies, we need to know the truth of our sins. We see something similar happening in slow motion with Peter.

The story of Peter's relationship with Jesus is one of the Bible's great love stories. In Luke's Gospel, Jesus calls Peter to discipleship but his recognition of Jesus' holiness is accompanied by the shocking realization of his own sinfulness, and he can think of nothing better than to ask Jesus to draw back from him. Jesus does not deny that Peter is a sinner, or wait for him to do penance, but immediately gives him a commission to fish for souls. The suggestion here is that the closer we come to Jesus in companionship, the more an awareness of our fragility will lead us to an overwhelming sense of God's mercy. As we trace Peter's progress through the Gospels we see him falling more deeply in love with Jesus, but also struggling to understand him and take on board the implications of his teaching. Led by his temperament to more than ordinary highs and lows, he makes great gestures of love and loyalty only to sink beneath the waves. Jesus calls him Rock, but he also calls him Satan, and, like all of us, he has elements of both within him. Finally the worst happens: he is indeed 'sifted like wheat', as Jesus predicted, and all that is on the surface falls apart, revealing to him in dreadful clarity the weak, sinful man that he is. This is a truly appalling realization. In Judas a similar realization leads to suicide, whereas for Peter the truth leads to agonized repentance and at last the abandonment of all his delusions of self-sufficiency.

'Blessed are those who know their need of God.' Peter at last knows his need of God to the very depths of himself, and is able to say with utmost sincerity, 'Lord, you know everything; you know that I love you' (John 21.17). This is almost like watching Peter go through the exercises of the First Week. His response at the end is one of honest acknowledgement of his inner poverty, but it is this that enables his declaration of love. It is no longer fuelled by a false sense of his own strength but by a sense of the utterly undeserved mercy he has received. Ignatius speaks of those who have understood this mystery in the innermost part of themselves as giving a cry of wonder at how, despite all their sins, they have been sustained by God and all creation. This is the cry of John Newton, the converted slave-trader, who sings of once being lost but now being found by 'amazing grace'. It is the cry of every truly repentant sinner. Such depths of gratitude and love cannot be felt by those who have only a vague sense of something not being quite right in their lives, which they ought to get round to doing something about at some point.

Questions for reflection or discussion

1 The First Week of the Ignatian Exercises is all about the amazing grace of knowing myself to be a loved and forgiven sinner. Look up the website:

<www.ignatianspirituality.com/ignatian-prayer/the-spiritual -exercises/an-ignatian-prayer-adventure>.

This is a whole online version of the Exercises, but you may like to read over the content of the Third Week. What do you learn about sin and forgiveness from this?

2 What do you understand by 'the divided self'? Have you ever experienced being divided from your truest self? How and why does that happen?

3 Look up the passages about Peter in the Gospels. Can you see any pattern emerging from his response to Jesus? What does it tell you about yourself in relation to Jesus?

7

Caught in the system

―――――・◆・―――――

Things fall apart; the centre cannot hold.
(W. B. Yeats)[1]

Lent, and the way of praying that we discover through the First Week of the Ignatian Exercises, does not just face us with our own sin but with the sinfulness of the systems in which we are all 'bound to sin' by our belonging in a world constructed on complex social, political and financial networks. We buy and use commodities produced by the sweated labour of others. Our high streets, shops and food outlets disguise the presence of modern-day slaves. Economic policies force the poor and those at risk to pay through cuts in public services for money squandered by those who are already rich and cushioned against trouble. Violence and warfare remain a daily reality for millions. For all our wonderful technological advances, we have not learned how to live without despoiling the earth or how to eradicate sickness and poverty for the majority of the world's population.

Statistics from the United Nations Sustainable Development Goals tell us that the wealth of the poorest half of the world's population has fallen by 38 per cent in the past 25 years. Every year 3 billion tonnes of food worth $1 trillion, an estimated one-third of all food produced worldwide, is wasted. Some 815 million people, including 200 million children, suffer malnutrition, while global obesity is on the rise and 38 million children are clinically obese or overweight. Yearly more than 5 million children die before their fifth birthday and 30 per cent of children remain out of school, while AIDS is the second most common cause of adolescent deaths globally. Worldwide, 3 in 10 people lack access to safe water and 6 in 10 to safe sanitation, while 1 billion people have no access to electricity.

Oceans contain 97 per cent of the earth's water, and represent 99 per cent of the planet's living space by volume. As much as 40 per cent of the world oceans are heavily affected by human activities, including pollution, depleted fisheries and loss of coastal habitats. Forests are home to more than 80 per cent of all terrestrial species of animals, plants and insects and some 70 million indigenous people. Due to drought and desertification each minute 23 hectares of land are lost.[2] This is what systemic sin looks like – a world in which millions of human beings and God's good creation fail to flourish as a result of unjust political, social and economic structures. It is as much a vision of hell as those provided by Ignatius in the First Week when he faces the individual retreatant with the consequences of personal sin.

Such statistics can induce in us a desolation and despondency that leads to paralysis, or they can galvanize us into action. At the end of a time of prayer Ignatius encourages us to engage in a 'colloquy' or personal conversation with God. At the beginning of the First Week he places us in our imaginations in front of Jesus crucified and moves us to ask, 'What response have I made to Christ? How do I respond to Christ now? What response should I make to Christ?' (*Sp.Exx.* 53).

Looking at the brokenness of our world we might be tempted to ask, 'What on earth can I do in the face of all this?' and decide that the answer is nothing. William Wilberforce had very few friends and allies when he began to campaign for the abolition of slavery in Britain in the eighteenth century. Britain's wealth was built on the slave trade. No one questioned it – not even figures of the Christian establishment, many of whom were involved, at a discreet distance, in slave ownership. Yet now no Christian could contemplate the idea that owning another human being like a piece of property is morally acceptable. Fragile and isolated individuals though we may feel ourselves to be, we can change the way whole countries and continents think and act. Wilberforce wrote:

> Things great have small beginnings.
> Every downpour is just a raindrop,
> Every fire is just a spark,
> Every harvest is just a seed,
> Every journey is just a step because
> Without that step there will be no journey,
> Without that raindrop there can be no shower,
> Without that seed there can be no harvest.[3]

Transforming the world is not simply an option for when we are feeling enthused and energetic. It is the direct and necessary response, however inadequate it may seem to us, embedded within our choice to turn from sin and follow Jesus. When he and his disciples are surrounded by a crowd of 5,000 hungry people, he says to them, 'You give them something to eat.' 'We have nothing here but five loaves and two fish' (Matt. 14.16–17), reply the horrified disciples – he can't surely be serious that this will be enough? And yet it proves to be more than enough when they put their trust in his power. In a talk given in Durham University in 2011 Cardinal Peter Turkson said:

> The 'outer ecology' of the structures of our family, our community and our society – what we call justice and peace or their absence – reflects the 'inner ecology' of each individual, community and organization. Individuals who refuse to change will contribute to the establishment or maintenance of unjust and conflictive societies. Those who promote peaceful transformation of the world in a convincing way have usually worked to transform violent and oppressive tendencies in themselves and have become advocates for those who are suffering the violent consequences of unjust structures.[4]

What is being said here is that we can be world-changers, but change is not a matter of what is 'out there'. It begins 'in here'. Ignatius invites us prayerfully to reflect on the ways in which we need fixing ourselves before we can try to fix the world. It is not about getting a new self-image or having a spiritual makeover. It is about doing the inner work so that we can be ready to do the outer work and make a real difference.

Radicalism is a dangerous word these days. It stands in the popular mind for mindless violence and cruelty in the name of religious extremism. We are rightly afraid of young people becoming radicalized, and increasing numbers of laws are being enacted to prevent that happening in schools, prisons and anywhere else that extreme religious ideas can get hold of vulnerable people. But the word 'radical' means 'at the roots'. Jesus invites us to change radically from the selfishness and egotism that is at the root of all human nature to an extremism of love – a love that does not seek to destroy the life of others but to give up our own life in loving service. The paradox is that by giving up our life in this way we receive it back a hundredfold, and discover what it is to be human beings fully alive.

Joining the revolution

Pope Francis is a Jesuit, and the spirit of Ignatius breathes through much of what he says and writes. One of his most often repeated words is 'tenderness'. In his Apostolic Exhortation *Evangelii Gaudium* (the Joy of the Gospel) he says: 'True faith in the incarnate Son of God is inseparable from self-giving, from membership in the community, from service, from reconciliation with others. The Son of God, by becoming flesh, summoned us to the revolution of tenderness.'[5] The Second Week of the Exercises is, in this sense, a revolutionaries' handbook. The tenderness of which Pope Francis speaks here is not some spiritual marshmallow, soft and squishy. From the very beginning of the Second Week we see that following in the way of Jesus costs 'not less than everything'.[6] Mary and Joseph accept the angel's message, which means the end of all their normal expectations of home, marriage and family life. Whatever it is going to be like to be the parents of the Messiah, the living Word of God, it is not going to be what they had previously dreamed of. We follow Jesus in his public life, from the temptations in the desert through to the demanding years of teaching and healing, and we see them as a series of confrontations with the pain of the world. Jesus' self-emptying love is expressed in taking the form of a servant (Phil. 2.7). We are invited to be alongside him, and as we become part of each encounter we find ourselves meeting Jesus personally and feeling in our own flesh and our own hearts a reaction to him that mirrors the reactions of others within the scene. Our wounds are touched with the lepers, blind Bartimaeus, the Gerasene demoniac. Our fear and self-doubt are met with compassion in the woman with the haemorrhage and the man with the possessed son. We struggle with our hard questions along with the Syro-Phoenician woman and Jairus, and we learn to have our understanding of God expanded as we sit at the well in Samaria.

In doing all this, we consider the call to discipleship and what it may cost us. Many of Ignatius' early companions were, relatively speaking, 'rich young men'. They were privileged and well educated and he invited them to give up all the status and protection that their station in life would normally afford them. They ended up trekking up mountains, through hostile territory and into miserable villages to minister to poor and ignorant people who did not always receive them with open arms. They sailed across seas to unknown lands to face cultures they had never encountered, or spent themselves in caring for the plague-stricken in filthy city slums and inadequate hospitals. Some of them spent long and frustrating hours trying to broker peace among Christians engaged in lethal religious wars, or pushing for reform in a church that was in desperate need of it. In all this they were trying to build a church worthy of the Holy Spirit that Jesus breathed into it in the Upper Room with his disciples. Pope Francis' vision for the Church has deep resonances of the Second Week, with its summons to be poor and compassionate with the poor, compassionate Christ. He says:

> The thing the church needs most today is the ability to heal wounds and to warm the hearts of the faithful; it needs nearness, proximity. I see the church as a field hospital after battle. It is useless to ask a seriously injured person if he has high cholesterol and about the level of his blood sugars! You have to heal his wounds. Then we can talk about everything else. Heal the wounds, heal the wounds . . . And you have to start from the ground up.[7]

He talks of preferring a church that is 'bruised, hurting and dirty because it has been out on the streets, rather than a Church which is unhealthy from being confined and from clinging to its own security'.[8] The invitation of the Second Week is to pray in such a way that we can be where Jesus is, seeing and feeling as he does and being drawn into doing things the Jesus way. This is not just a spiritual flight of fancy – it is gritty and gutsy and very real. Pope Francis speaks of getting close enough to people that we can touch the suffering flesh of Christ in others and take on the 'smell of the sheep'.[9]

The Second Week contains a number of 'set-piece' meditations where we are faced repeatedly with the self-giving that is characteristic of Jesus himself and that becomes the characteristic of those who follow him. The question facing us is, 'How are we going to choose to follow?' In contemplating Christ the King and his call, we pray not to be unwilling or unable to hear him, but to be ready and willing to do his will. Ignatius imagines an earthly king summoning companions in a heroic enterprise, and then imagines Jesus inviting us to share in all his labours and hardships in the great undertaking of conquering evil. The language is that of the chivalry of Ignatius' youth. In these days of the media exposure of world leaders and celebrities with their feet of clay, this language may not appeal to a modern audience. In other parts of the Exercises Ignatius' gender-related comments can also fall awkwardly on third-millennium ears. There has been excellent work done on reclaiming the Exercises for an audience with different sensibilities, but the core dynamic of what Ignatius writes remains as compelling now as it did in his own day.[10]

Amazing grace

What is called the dynamic of the Exercises works in an organic way. Beyond all our need to control our lives and determine our own futures, we learn that love is the driving force in the world and we respond to God's initiative to know that love in our deepest core. From the starting point of that unshakeable knowledge we are led into a process of self-discovery, learning God's answer to the question, 'Who do you say that I am?' Inevitably the answer we get is an honest one, and the light of God's love may throw into strong relief some dark places within ourselves. But the truth of our own existence is revealed to us at the same time as the reality of God's amazing grace, forgiving, strengthening and sustaining.

Ignatius constantly reminds us to pray for what we desire and to become accustomed to exploring our deepest longings, as this is where the Spirit of God is at work within us. For Ignatius prayer begins with us placing ourselves in God's presence, asking for what we deeply want and encountering God in the Scriptures in a way that opens us up to being transformed as those who met Jesus were transformed. Like them we sometimes come to this encounter with conflicting needs and attitudes: 'I believe, help my unbelief!' Our deep desires may be thwarted at the start by fears, moods, self-judging anxieties, self-protecting untruths. Exposure to the loving and challenging presence of Jesus may help us to understand more clearly the interplay of God's desires within us and our unconscious defences. Prayer ends with a conversation that becomes a progressive dynamic of self-gift. This attitude of sincerity and transparency, Mary Ward's 'that we be such as we appear and appear such as we are', is the prerequisite for choices large and small that open out before us. They may not lead us to a specific act like moving house or making a lifetime decision such as getting married or embarking on a career. They may, rather, lead us to a 'how', learning to be ourselves in the same context but in a different way that is more life-giving. It may be about having our perspective adjusted so that we come to look on the world with different eyes and engage with it in radically different ways. Above all, this way of praying gradually gives us the courage to trust God and the gifts that God has given us. Many old-fashioned prayer books taught us to make acts of faith, hope and love, expressing our trust in God. Here we experience them in reverse, hearing God say to us, 'I believe in you, I have hopes for you, I trust and love you – so now what shall we do together in the world?'

Questions for reflection or discussion

1 What do you understand by 'systemic sin'? How do you see yourself as trying to live and act for the common good?
2 Pope Francis talks about our need to be people who can 'heal wounds and warm the hearts of the faithful'. How might you, in your personal circumstances, go about this?
3 Read Matthew 25.31–46. What do you understand Jesus to be saying about how we are to live in relation to others? Take any newspaper and read the first few pages. How do they seem when set alongside this passage?

8

Surveying the wondrous cross

———◆———

O King of the Friday
Whose limbs were stretched on the Cross,
O Lord who did suffer
The bruises, the wounds, the loss,
We stretch ourselves
Beneath the shield of thy might,
Some fruit from the tree of thy passion
Fall on us this night!
(Ancient Irish)

The Scripture readings for Lent lead us inevitably to the Passion and bring us face to face with the price that Jesus paid to liberate us from all that makes us and the whole cosmos less than the marvel God created us to be. Some people undergoing the Spiritual Exercises make a particular choice or election as part of the Second Week. For others it is more a reorientation of their lives and what Ignatius calls their 'way of proceeding', which means their normal way of functioning. Whether we stand on the threshold of a major decision or we are looking at the reconfiguration of our outlook on and engagement with life, as companions of Jesus we look to him as the compass for our life and take our bearings from his death and resurrection as the starting point for living life to the full.

Christians have very different ways of reacting to the death and resurrection of Jesus. Some lay such agonized emphasis on his sufferings that they seem almost to get stuck there. In some countries churches are packed to the gills on Good Friday but significantly emptier on Easter Sunday. A gloomy faith, fixated on suffering, can lead to a repressive and judgemental outlook on life that allows no room for the extraordinary miracle of Jesus' resurrection and the transformation of the whole of creation that is its fruit. At the same time, a faith that is only Easter Sunday and hallelujahs can fail to

63

take seriously the very real struggles that even dedicated followers of Jesus may encounter, and can appear glibly optimistic and superficial in its engagement with the crucifixion of Christ that continues in his desperately suffering people and God's desecrated creation.

Jesus' sufferings can act as a litmus test for our self-understanding and our ability to cope with the mystery of human weakness. Many people praying through the Exercises or through experiences typical of the Third Week find at this stage that they come up against their own fragility. Like Peter, James and John they want to stay close to Jesus in the hour of need, but find themselves falling asleep physically, emotionally or spiritually. Their hopes of being swept up in some great wave of tragic feelings descend into the banality of an imagination that simply will not function, or a will that cannot be bent in the required direction, or a wall of dull emotional indifference. There are many reasons for this, some of which are about our unconscious need to avoid unpleasant or frightening or unhappy thoughts. There is also the struggle, for some, with their own remembered pain and loss, and what can emerge is a deep anger with God that is triggered by coming close to the death of God's only Son. The God who allows Jesus to die in this way and who appears indifferent to our own sufferings can seem like a joyless monster who devours sacrifice and demands a tribute of blood. In the face of the appalling suffering that screams from our television and computer screens every day, we can feel a deadening sense of cynicism and frustration at a God who seems unwilling or unable to help in any effective way. Praying in Third Week mode takes us to the very bedrock of our faith and doubt and reminds us in the starkest way possible that we are not ultimately in control, either of our own lives or of the universe.

Human suffering and evil are the stumbling block on which many people's faith founders. Praying through the Passion of Jesus may draw us close to some kind of acceptance and dim understanding of God's response to our suffering. But it may also challenge our capacity to keep on believing and hoping. Thoughts and feelings that we have repressed as unworthy of a person of faith may surface, but, painful though they are, this can be a sign of grace beginning to emerge. This kind of prayer, where we confront our bewilderment and pain at what we experience as the remoteness of God, is far more real than easy protestations of love and loyalty that cover up what we find unbearable. This is the prayer of Peter and the disciples when their sincerely meant but empty promises of fidelity crashed down on them in their fear and faithlessness, as the reality of what redemption meant for Jesus confronted them.

For others, the cross of Christ becomes the only hope, as it can never be separated from the resurrection. They are two sides of the same coin, two facets of the same mystery into which we are drawn, so that we experience the one total mystery at work in ourselves and in our world. This is where the early revelation of ourselves as sinful and beloved becomes thoroughly physical and concrete. If we can bring ourselves to engage with this mystery, we can be left in no doubt that truly neither life nor death nor any created thing will be able to separate us from the love of God that is in Christ Jesus our Lord (Rom. 8.38–39).

Feeling the pain

Ignatius encourages us to ask for the grace of having deep feelings of sorrow and shame in the face of Jesus' sufferings for our sins. Again, this could become yet another opportunity to wallow in self-loathing and futile sentimentality, or it could more fruitfully lead us into the feelings of his companions. But we should not be surprised by the whole spectrum of those feelings. In the face of terrible loss and pain some people are engulfed by unbearable feelings, while others switch off emotionally and go numb. Some go into hectic rescue mode, while others sink into apathy. So when we are in the midst of Third Week experiences, or we are praying in companionship with the suffering Jesus, we may react at either end of this spectrum. For his disciples, the sufferings of Jesus were a mirror in which they came at last to see the shallowness of their commitment and the self-seeking that lay behind all their avowals of love and loyalty. If we ask to be given the heart of a true disciple, then we can expect to feel as they felt, faced with the terrible blow of Jesus' arrest, trial and death. If we follow them through the journey to Jerusalem, to the cleansing of the Temple, the escalation of hostility from the religious establishment, the Last Supper with its shocking message in the washing of feet and the sharing of bread and wine, on to the garden of Gethsemane, the public trial and its terrible outcome, we should not be surprised if we are overcome by feelings of numbness, desperate avoidance, the desire to run away and a sheer lack of comprehension.

We ask to share in Jesus' own sorrow, which he himself called a 'sorrow unto death'. Being alongside a friend who is suffering requires true selflessness on our part. There is nothing worse than trying to share with someone a personal tragedy or deep sorrow only to receive back the fatuous comment 'I know how you feel', or for them to try to cap our story with a worse one of their own. No one knows how another person feels because our feelings are unique to us. If we are drowning in pain and sadness it does not help to be told that some other vessel has been shipwrecked and gone down with all hands. Compassion literally means 'suffering with', so this is a time for us to engage in selfless prayer, asking only for the grace to stay with Jesus, even if we have no words to offer and our thoughts and feelings fail us. What he asked of his dearest friends in Gethsemane was that they stay with him, not just in the sense of remaining physically but in the sense of hanging on in there with him. Anyone who has had to sit long hours by the bedside of a loved one who is suffering or dying will know that there is often nothing we can offer but our sheer presence, and that is all they want and need. This is probably not the moment for lengthy explanations or discussions but for silent willingness to persevere. As Jesus looked down from the cross he will have seen his mother and the other women doing nothing but stand silently around him. This is the prayer of the Passion – we're here because we're here.

It is a deeply transformative way of praying, but one whose work is done in the silence of our hearts and is not always visible to our conscious mind. In Jesus' suffering and death we see God willingly take on all the frustration and futility of the human ego. All the actors in the drama of his death: Judas, Pilate, Herod, Peter, the religious establishment in Jerusalem, are models of human self-centredness, obtuseness and hardness of heart. At the beginning of the First Week, in Ignatius' contemplation on the Incarnation, he imagines the Trinity looking down on the world, taking stock of the disorder and pain within it and deciding to send the Son to redeem the human race from within. From that moment on we are invited to enter into the eternal community of love that is God, Father, Son and Spirit. It is by entering more deeply into that primordial loving relationship that we discover the full extent of God's tenderness and compassion for sinful and suffering humanity.

A singular freedom

In her mature years Mary Ward found herself travelling around Europe, leading growing numbers of companions who felt called like her to serve God in the world through the spiritual heritage given to Ignatius. This caused significant difficulties in a church and a secular society unable to believe that God could truly call women in this way.[1] In 1615 Mary received an insight while making the Exercises that offered her an understanding of what it might be like to have been freed from disordered attachments. She calls it a clear and perfect state, not one of mystical ecstasies but of 'singular freedom' from every tendency to cling to what is not God, becoming available for whatever God might ask. She goes on to speak of this inner freedom as making a person able to 'refer all to God'. This seems to her to be similar to the state of Adam and Eve in paradise before the fall, a state restored to humanity by grace alone in which nothing can separate us from the love of God in Christ. Every aspect of human and material existence becomes the place where the glory of God finds a home. There is no experience too trivial or too terrible, too blissful or too banal, that God cannot be found within it. This is the 'glorious freedom of the children of God', the union between ourselves and God and the whole universe which comes from the transformation won by Christ in his resurrection (Rom. 8.19–23). Mary sees this restored relationship expressed in justice and sincerity:

> That word 'Justice', and those in former times that were called just persons, works of justice, done in innocence, and that we be such as we appear and appear such as we are: these things often since occurred to my mind with a liking for them.[2]

It is important to remember that the whole of Ignatius' gaze within the Exercises and therefore within ordinary, daily prayer is fixed on our imitating Jesus, the eternal Word of God who emptied himself in order to assume the condition of a slave (Phil. 2.7). While the focused or daily work of such prayer is very much at the level of the inner self, it has an outward orientation towards the world. So coming close to Jesus in his humiliation and suffering means coming close to the humiliation and suffering of all the least of his brothers and sisters. It means being willing to have our heart broken by the relentless injustices and indignities that are the daily bread of so many, so that for ever after we might have a heart of flesh and not of stone that is turned towards them and active for their good. In a compassion-fatigued culture, where the worst miseries the world can offer get barely a glance in the morning news, we are taken with Jesus to the very abyss of horror and suffering so that we can learn to struggle with Christ playing in ten thousand million places in limbs and eyes not his.[3] That is the hard-won gift of becoming hungry and thirsty for justice, which comes to us through praying the Passion and resurrection of Jesus. It means that we will never again be able to look on personal or systemic injustice and remain unresponsive.

Rules for eating

One thing that is generally known about Lent, even by those for whom it has no other contextual meaning, is that it is about giving things up and fasting. This is often seen purely in terms of self-denial and self-discipline, but Ignatius sees it as having a broader and altogether more positively oriented meaning. At the end of the Third Week of the Spiritual Exercises, which begins with the Last Supper and ends with Christ's death and burial in the tomb, Ignatius slips in a curious little page called 'Rules with Regard to Eating'. They are easily overlooked by retreatants and guides alike, perhaps uncomfortable with the medieval feel of it all. But Ignatius did nothing by chance, and this page lies at the heart both of the Exercises and of the Passion itself, because it is all about how we deal with disordered appetites at source.

In the past decade, deaths from liver disease in the UK have risen by around 25 per cent. Of those deaths, 90 per cent occurred among the under-70s and many of them among the under-40s. In our prisons, record numbers of people are serving life sentences for murders committed under the influence of alcohol rather than under the influence of drugs. We are binge drinking ourselves and other people to death. We are also eating ourselves to death. Statistics show that over 60 per cent of adults and 30 per cent of children are overweight: 1 in 4 adults in England are classified as obese, with as many as 30,000 people dying prematurely every year from obesity-related conditions. 'The road of excess leads to the palace of wisdom,' says William Blake in his *Proverbs of Hell*; and 'You never know what is enough unless you know what is more than enough.'[4] The trouble, it seems, is that we don't know what is more than enough, or, if we do, we cannot or will not do anything about it. If the road of excess does in any way lead to the palace of wisdom, the danger is that we will be too inebriated to walk straight and too fat to fit through the doorway once we get there.

But Ignatius' primary purpose is not to get us all into physical or even spiritual shape. It is to provide an effective way of praying and living with the totality of ourselves, in an outward sign of the inward grace that we are desiring, which is true freedom of heart. Ignatius himself was no stranger to fasting-induced illness and conceded later in life that this can be a form of compulsive disorder. Using the power of the imagination he emphasizes the harmony and order that come with making balance and restraint the stuff of our daily living. He advocates a process that he calls in Latin *agere contra*, which is the idea that pulling gently in the opposite direction of an impulse run wild helps us to regain our balance.[5] It connects with the very first paragraph of the Exercises, with its talk of 'preparing and disposing the soul to rid itself of all disordered attachments' in order better to seek and find the will of God and with it the fullness of human flourishing.

Throughout the Exercises, as throughout the Gospel narratives, runs the thread of making choices. We see the choices we make, both great and small, in the light of those made by Jesus, all of which are the choices of a foolish God whose folly is wiser than our wisdom and who displays power through letting it go. Our world is in thrall at the systemic level to unsustainable consumption. We are all enmeshed in the economic systems that both create and are the product of the consumer juggernaut. They thrive on the drivenness of those whose daily grinding toil makes it possible for the minority world to live beyond its need, and the drivenness of those who are straining to maintain an unsustainable lifestyle bloated by affluence.

The consumer culture and the driven lifestyles adopted by many as the price of living within it produce a whole array of addictive and compulsive habits. If these happen at the level of the body, so must our counter-cultural spiritual habits. Eating is hugely problematic for women dominated by the body image insisted upon by the fashion culture and, for both genders, food is often deeply embedded within our routine compensation mechanisms. Though generally not an addiction in the proper sense, eating can get out of control, becoming a habit dominated by compulsion. Food has the added challenge of being the one thing on which we cannot go cold turkey. We have to eat to live, even if we struggle to know and control the difference between what is enough and what is more than enough.

In the Fourth Week, retreatants emerge into the focus on resurrection and the power of the Spirit within life as it stretches before them. The idea of this kind of spiritual space is to incarnate as fully as possible an experience of prayer that sees those praying stripped of deeply embedded illusions and compulsions and liberated towards being able to choose, on a daily basis, the end for which God created them. This finds expression in transformative discipleship in whatever way of life best presents itself. It has implications for how we live, down to the smallest detail.

So the rules for eating are about both penance and temperance, but also about liberation. Ignatius notes that the principal reason for doing penance is to make satisfaction for our sins, to overcome disordered appetites and to obtain some grace or gift earnestly desired. At the heart of penance lies a lucid knowledge of what drives our disordered lives. Such insight is a gift worth praying and fasting for. The dysfunctional appetite of many may not be for food but for power, money, status, image, success, addictive work patterns, fun: illusory needs in pursuit of illusory ambitions, all of which involve fleeing from the truth of ourselves. The compulsive compensation mechanisms that kill the pain of modern living may be television, sport, the internet, shopping, even the pursuit of the spiritual as if it were a lifestyle choice or accessory. We need liberating from these as much as from any other drive that has us in its grip. The crucifixion of Jesus stripped his followers bare of many illusions and gave them an insight into the extent of their own poverty so that they could become rich in God's grace. Ignatius' Exercises put us in touch, at the level of feeling and imagination, but also at the level of our senses and our living flesh, with the dynamic of our own operative mechanisms. It is this truth that we try to get in touch with during Lent, with a view to seeing ourselves more clearly through the power of the risen Christ.

The resurrection appearances are a further process in shedding illusions, even the most cherished illusion of how God characteristically operates. The disciples of Christ crucified and risen become able to see themselves and their place in the general order of creation with the compassionate eyes of the loving Creator. It becomes possible to live in the way of the resurrection, learning to be led in willing poverty of spirit, against the grain of the drive for control, security and self-gratification. This becomes part of the liberation of the earth itself from its subjection to the futility of our unsustainable ambitions and consumer desires.

For many the term 'self-denial' is problematic, because it sounds like a form of self-harm. In fact we are talking about the enrichment of self that comes when we are no longer at the mercy of our appetites. I am not denying my self when I resist my appetites; I am denying my self when I indulge any compulsive appetite. Nietzsche thought of Christianity as self-denial, masochism and the sadism of enjoying watching people suffer. In those terms the ultimate sacrifice of Christ or the martyr and the small sacrifices of the penitent are seen as the inflicting of punishment. But Ignatius saw the reordering of the appetites as a route to self-knowledge and to liberation from compulsions. Like prayer, it deserves to be something that is woven into the fabric of our lives all the time rather than being dusted down once in a liturgical while.

----•◆•----

Questions for reflection or discussion

1 Read chapter 14 of the Gospel of Mark. What do you notice about different people's reactions to the prospect of Jesus' sufferings? What do you feel when you read this passage?
2 Mary Ward speaks of the need to 'refer all to God'. What do you understand by this?
3 Ignatius speaks of self-denial in the Exercises and acting against disordered attachments. How do you react to this idea? Is there anything in your life that you would like to turn from?

9

An attitude of gratitude

————•◦•————

*Be confident in God, and more than ever grateful to his unseen
goodness.*   (Mary Ward)

The culmination of Lent is Holy Week, when we walk with Jesus to
the very foot of the cross. It sometimes seems as if the solemnity and
sorrow of the Good Friday service is barely over when it's straight to
the bustle of putting flowers and candles on the altar, gold and white
replacing penitential purple and Easter Sunday beginning in antici-
pation. Both psychologically and spiritually this is to sell ourselves
short of the true process of going down into the tomb with Jesus
on Holy Saturday. When people make the Ignatian Exercises in the
30-day mode they are often encouraged not to pray, not to go near
the Scriptures or a church or specifically holy space, and actually
experience the sense of emptiness and loss that this can give them.
He is truly dead, and the physical companionship of the days on the
road is over. If we do not feel in the depths of ourselves that Jesus is
actually dead, we will not feel anything very distinct when we find
that he has risen.

The icons beloved of the Eastern traditions of Christianity contain
a strong theological symbolism. In depictions of the descent of the
risen Jesus into hell, Jesus stands between two tombs from which he
pulls out Adam on one side and Eve on the other from the darkness
of death. Beneath his feet are usually the gates of hell, which he has
burst open and flattened. A large collection of locks, chains and keys
populate hell, and beneath Jesus' feet is a figure, bound and chained.
It is the adversary, the Accuser of the book of Revelation, who has
been thrown down for ever. The chains symbolize both the length of
time that the patriarchs and matriarchs of the Old Testament have
languished in Hades, the land of shadow, and also all that keeps us
under lock and key in the sense of our imprisonment in sinful and
death-dealing ways of being.

The risen Jesus tramples down all the symbols of our captivity. We easily bind ourselves in attitudes and patterns of thought and behaviour that are deadly to us, locking ourselves in by convincing ourselves that there is no way out. We are right, in the sense that, using our own strength, there is none. Salvation is not an exercise in self-help. We need it precisely because we so easily fall into traps and then compound them by our inability to forgive ourselves for our fragilities. The book of Exodus reminds us that God's great saving act for the Israelites was to rescue them from bondage. Today we talk more easily about addiction, or toxic habits, but the effects are the same. Jesus is first and foremost a liberator who reaches into the tombs we build for ourselves to pull us out. But this does not generally happen in an instant. Even Paul, after his blindingly sudden experience of conversion on the road to Damascus, had many subsequent conversions where he had to learn to outgrow old patterns, to move and to change when it became clear that spiritual growth was calling him on.

We live in a world that cannot wait. Modern advertising speak has made the word 'grab' acceptable. Grab 'n' Go, Grab on the Run, Grab a Bite – all this is about snatching food or some other necessary commodity while hurtling off to do something else, never taking time to savour and relish. Both 'savour' and 'relish' are words frequently used by Ignatius. The spiritual tradition he made famous is all about being contemplatives in action, but the way we make our action contemplative is to be present in the moment and not to see time, or the passing of time, as an enemy to be conquered. Ignatius encourages us to savour and relish the word of God, or the moment of awareness, and stay with it until it has done its work. In prayer we often find ourselves having to 'wait on God'. This can be immensely frustrating when God seems to have fallen asleep at the prow of the boat, doing nothing as we sink beneath the storm. Allowing ourselves a proper Holy Saturday or 'Tomb Day' experience in prayer is often a matter of learning to wait, but it also means trusting in the one who tramples on all the locks and chains that bind us, pulling us out of the dark places where we are unable to see clearly the healing and liberating work as it unfolds. God's goodness is sometimes unseen, but no less good for that.

Ignatius made a remarkable inner journey from the soldier of fortune determined on self-advancement to the poor and humble pilgrim who put his entire life in God's hands and asked only to be 'placed with his Son'. In all his writings he sets great store by humility. His biographer, the tireless Gonçalves da Câmara, tells us:

> I remember that once when we were speaking about a good religious whom he knew and I said that he was a man of much prayer, the Father [Ignatius] altered my remark and said: 'He is a man of much mortification.'[1]

Mortification is a very old-fashioned word and has resonances of a dessicated ascetic, sitting in a darkened corner gnawing on a bone while others eat their fill. This is far from Ignatius' meaning. He uses the word to describe someone who has come to true inner freedom. His comment to da Câmara suggests that such an internalized habit is of greater importance to him than hours in prayer. It is not more important than prayer, as such, it *is* prayer and the true fruit of prayer to the one whom Pope Francis calls the 'God of little things', the everyday God to whom we refer everything. Self-knowledge and a healthy sense of balance are always the hallmarks here.

A young Jesuit had become seriously ill and wrote to Ignatius asserting that it was his determination to do away with sensuality in himself that had made him ill. Ignatius himself was not far from death, but his advice is notable for its humane and down-to-earth directness. While acknowledging that there is merit in suppressing all inclinations leading to sin and away from God's will, even while ill, he also warns against 'immoderate and unseasonable' mental exercise. There is a right time for mortification, but such repressions are not for everyone or for every occasion: 'In fact there are times when, in order to sustain one's strength over the long haul in God's service, it is more meritorious to take some honest recreation for the senses than to repress them.'[2]

In this sense mortification is synonymous with humility and freedom, but here again Ignatius gives an old-fashioned word new meaning. One of the most villainous figures in literary history is Uriah Heep from Charles Dickens's *David Copperfield*. He constantly stresses his humility and his respect for his employers, but all the while he is seething with envy and thwarted ambition, and scheming for the downfall of those whose better fortune he hates and resents. This is not the humility we find in Ignatius himself or in his writings, nor is it the humility we find in the Scriptures. God says of Moses, 'he is entrusted with all my house. With him I speak face to face' (Num. 12.7–8), yet elsewhere it is said of Moses, this unique man who has seen God's face and lived, that he is the humblest man on earth. So closeness to God and humility appear to go hand in hand. Far from nurturing secret grandiose thoughts, Moses knows his own weakness. When first called by God he begs to have the burden of leadership passed on to his brother Aaron who is a much better speaker. Moses knows his limitations, but God calls him to collaborate in the work of saving Israel, despite his shortcomings. His siblings resent his favoured position, but God champions Moses not for his superior virtues but for his openness to intimate relationship with his Creator. There is no trace of sycophantic self-abasement here or need to put up a polite front when speaking to God. Moses is very real with God, saying exactly what he thinks and feels. This, says God, is the meaning of being 'at home in my house'.

If we are open to sharing our real selves in intimate relationship with God we can also be at home in the house of one whom Mary Ward called her 'Parent of parents and Friend of friends'. Peter has a relationship with Jesus similar to Moses' relationship with God. He is mostly at home in Jesus' house, but his approach to their friendship can swing between impulsive generosity and fearful withdrawal. Whether sinking into the lake or denying Jesus at his Passion, Peter's weaknesses are all too obvious, but so is his willingness to keep trying to follow his beloved Master faithfully. It is when he comes at last to know the extent of his own fragility and stops trying to keep hold of control that he learns what true discipleship means. It is not a performance-related activity but an openness to learning how to love beyond or despite our limitations. God sees into our hearts, and knows our deepest desires and motivations. If we can be our honest selves with God, at home in our Father's house, God will speak to us face to face. Ignatius tells us that humility is not the same as self-abasement. To make self-belittling comments in the style of Uriah Heep is to show ingratitude for God's gifts. When someone seems to have a high opinion of herself we sometimes ask, 'Who does she think she is – God's gift?' The correct answer is yes, we are, each and every one of us, God's gift to the world. But this is a cause for humble gratitude rather than for self-aggrandisement. Gratitude is at the heart of true humility, for it is our response in appreciation for God's gifts that leads us to turn in wonder and loving thanks to the giver of the gift. A person who becomes able to thank God daily for every gift, however small, starting from the gift of life itself, becomes increasingly alive to the endless, if often barely visible, signs of God's loving, grace-giving presence at every moment. A mortified person, in this sense, is fully aware of his limitations and even more fully aware of the extent of God's mercy, 'new every morning'. The gratitude that brims over from knowing this is expressed in a humility that focuses on God's compassion and amazing grace rather than on our failures to measure up to our own standards.

Saying 'Thank You'

The great set piece contemplation of the Fourth Week of the Spiritual Exercises is called the 'Contemplation for Attaining Love' or *Contemplatio*. The phrase in Spanish is *Contemplación para alcanzar amor*. We find the verb *alcanzar* in Teresa of Avila's prayer, 'Let Nothing Disturb You', in which she says:

> Let nothing disturb you,
> Nothing frighten you,
> All things are passing away:
> God never changes.
> Patience attains (*alcanza*) all things.
> Whoever has God lacks nothing,
> God alone suffices.[3]

This sense of attaining here and in the *Contemplatio* is not about grabbing or somehow earning through our own efforts, but receiving in gratitude through God's open-handed generosity. The *Contemplatio* has strong similarities with the Principle and Foundation at the beginning of the Exercises and brings us full circle back to where we began the pilgrimage with Ignatius. It is, structurally speaking, the fulfilment of the Principle and Foundation. It takes us back to the creation of the world and enables us to see ourselves as gifted from the beginning with being chosen and created by God, unique and graced. It enables us to see our personal history as part of salvation history, whatever the details of our story. It gives us a sense of our true place within the universe as partners rather than dominators of all else that lives. Above all it inspires us to an overwhelming sense of gratitude for what has been, what is and what is to come.

The word 'Eucharist' means the equivalent of 'thank you'. It comes as something of a shock to the sensibilities of one brought up in the Church of the West to hear the word used so casually in modern Greek. Heard at every turn on buses, in shops and in conversations between friends and strangers, *efharisto* is a common word in any person-to-person exchange. What effect might it have on our understanding of the Eucharist if for a day we exchanged the word 'Eucharist' for our usual use of 'thank you'? Apart from attracting some strange looks it might enable us to give greater importance to the gifts we perceive in every aspect of creation, as well as the gifts of kindness and attention we receive from one another as indicators that the living Christ is among us and present to us in all that surrounds us. It might also enable us to see the Eucharist itself as something more immediate and alive in the ordinary, so that living eucharistically as the body of Christ might take on a whole new meaning.

In the old translation of the Latin Mass the dismissal at the end was 'Go, the Mass is ended'. It is a terrible mistranslation of *Ite, missa est*. It suggests, 'Go back to your real lives, the holy bit is over for the week.' But the Latin verb *mitto* means to send, so the real meaning is 'Go, you've been sent', or 'Go, the Mass (the sending) has begun'. The Greek word for apostle comes from the word for being sent. In this sense the Eucharist is the blessing and strength from which we are sent out as modern apostles to be Christ in the world, meeting him and doing for him what we do for the least of our sisters and brothers. Many people see Ignatian spirituality as principally aimed at working on the inner self. But this would be pointless were it not fundamentally oriented towards the self in relationship with the outer world. More than anything else it is a spirituality of discipleship, a school of growth for those who have fallen in love with Jesus and answered his call. It is Mary Ward's 'freedom to refer all to God'.

This is articulated in a passage attributed to Pedro Arrupe (1907–91), who was leader of the Jesuits in the aftermath of the Second Vatican Council:

Nothing is more practical than
finding God, than
falling in Love
in a quite absolute, final way.
What you are in love with,
what seizes your imagination, will affect everything.
It will decide
what will get you out of bed in the morning,
what you do with your evenings,
how you spend your weekends,
what you read, whom you know,
what breaks your heart,
and what amazes you with joy and gratitude.
Fall in love, stay in love,
and it will decide everything.[4]

Living sacramentally – noticing the gift

If there are many opportunities for us to live more eucharistically in everyday life there are also repeated moments each day for us to live reconciliation, healing and anointing in the Spirit by being more attentive to the signs of our need for them. Martin Luther taught the 'priesthood of all believers'. The Latin word for priest is *pontifex*, which means bridge-builder. Our baptismal call invites us to build bridges of faith, hope and love in a world that for many is isolating and comfortless. Our every relationship of love and human solidarity builds bridges between people who are divided from one another in alienation and loneliness.

The mystery or 'sacrament' of God's presence hidden in the circumstances of any given 'now' is explored in a work attributed to the eighteenth-century French Jesuit Jean Pierre de Caussade, which speaks of the 'sacrament of the present moment'.[5] It can be easy to live this mystery when life makes sense to us and treats us with a measure of coherence, but well-nigh impossible when life's fragility overwhelms us and we find ourselves drowning in a sea of trouble and unable to trust in God's loving care. Faith as 'the assurance of things hoped for, the conviction of things not seen' (Heb. 11.1) is the only thing on which we can rely in such circumstances. It is that faith and the balance achieved by the grace Ignatius calls 'indifference' that enables us to let go of the need for security and control and place our lives in God's hands.

Ignatius gives us a prayer within this contemplation on the God who becomes present to us when we recognize the gifts that have been lavished upon us. It is called the *Suscipe*, after the first word in the Latin version:

> Take, Lord, and receive all my liberty, my memory, my understanding, and my entire will – all that I have and call my own. You have given it all to me. To you, Lord, I return it. Everything is yours; do with it what you will. Give me only your love and your grace. That is enough for me. (*Sp.Exx. 234*)

Ignatius tells us that love is about more than making enthusiastic professions of devotion. It is eminently practical. 'Love ought to show itself in deeds over and above words.' He goes on to say:

> Love consists in a mutual sharing of goods . . . as a lover one gives and shares with the beloved something of one's own personal gifts or some possession which one has or is able to give; so, too, the beloved shares in a similar way with the lover. (*Sp.Exx.* 231)

In a song based on this prayer, Jesuit songwriter Tom McGuinness writes the refrain, 'I know the gift is freely given, hard to understand, and I know the gift can only be returned.'[6]

We 'return' the gift not in the sense of giving it back because we don't want it, or we want a different, shinier model, but because it is the only fitting way we can show our gratitude, by understanding that every gift God gives us is given for the world, through our use of it for the reign of God.[7] Using gifts for their God-given purpose is truly to be grateful. If each present moment is a gift from God, then each 'now' can be lived to the full as a prayer of just return and gratitude. The *Suscipe* makes an interesting comparison with another prayer often (incorrectly) attributed to Ignatius:

> Dearest Jesus, teach me to be generous,
> Teach me to serve you as you deserve:
> To give and not to count the cost,
> To fight and not to heed the wounds,
> To toil and not to seek for rest,
> To labour and not to ask for any reward
> Save that of knowing that I do your will.[8]

There is passion and great generosity in this prayer, but there is also a whiff of the superhero. The subject of most of the verbs is, implicitly or explicitly, Me. This heroic and generous 'I' is still in some senses the centre of its own universe, and has not learned to acknowledge its limitations. Were it to have been written by Ignatius it would be the impulsive Ignatius setting off to Jerusalem to do great deeds for Christ. In the *Suscipe* the subject of most of the verbs is God. This is the prayer of the pilgrim Ignatius who has learned his own limitations, and the infinite possibilities that unfold when we learn to refer all to God, placing control and initiative back into God's hands. He returns all the gifts so as to learn to do with them what God wills. The clay is in the potter's hands rather than trying to turn the wheel by itself. The *Contemplatio* is often translated into English as above, 'give me only your love and your grace'. But the original Spanish is more correctly translated as 'give me only love of you'.[9] Even the capacity to love God is God's gift to us, and can only be returned.

Questions for reflection or discussion

1 How do you understand humility? How do you see it as helping people to be 'at home in God's house'?

2 Look up the icon of Jesus' descent into hell:

   <www.orthodoxroad.com/wp-content/uploads/2012/12/resurrection2007.jpg>.

   What do the locks and chains represent to you? How does it feel to see the risen Jesus trample on them?

3 Look at the two 'prayers of St Ignatius' quoted above. How do you react to each of them? Could you write your own personal prayer of offering?

Conclusion
Finding God in all things

———◆◈◆———

During these days of Lent we have walked with Ignatius, Mary Ward and others who have been part of the Ignatian family that has spread throughout the world in all the years since Ignatius' death in 1556. Even in his lifetime, as in that of Mary Ward, there were numerous attempts to modify their spiritual insights in the belief that they needed correcting. Mostly this was because their notion of God and a prayerful relationship with God seemed far too ordinary. A Jesuit, Francisco Onfroy, began to call for reform within the Jesuits, insisting that they could only be thought faithful and effective disciples of Jesus if they spent long hours in prayer. Ignatius writes a long letter outlining why he thinks that this is not true. Prayer needs, he says, to be balanced by deeds of love and service:

> The fact is that there are times when God is served more by other things than by prayer, so much so that for their sake God is happy that prayer be relinquished – and all the more that it be shortened.[1]

We get echoes of this when Ignatius writes about the younger Jesuit students immersed in their studies to their superior who is worried that this is taking their minds away from God: 'The occupation of the mind with academic pursuits naturally tends to produce a certain dryness in the interior affections. However, when the study is directed purely to God's service, it is an excellent devotion.'[2] He is not saying that neglecting prayer is unimportant or that study is a substitute for prayer, but 'whatever you do, in word or deed, do everything in the name of the Lord Jesus, giving thanks to God the Father through him' (Col. 3.17).

This is an important thing for us to take in: that any activity can in and of itself become a spiritual exercise if in a heartfelt and determined way it is done in and for Christ. Few of us have the luxury or even perhaps the inclination to spend long daily hours in prayer, but in this sense our day-to-day lives become a prayer. In an article entitled 'Love and Attention' theologian Janet Martin Soskice discusses the idea that whatever commands our attention and love identifies both who we are and what we should be: 'To be fully human and moral is to respond to that which demands or compels our response – the other attended to with love.'[3] She goes on to discuss the concept of the 'received spirituality' and theological perspective of the spiritual person and the spiritual life, which focuses on 'long periods of quiet, focused reflections, dark churches and dignified liturgies . . . time spent in contemplative prayer, guided or solitary retreats, and sometimes . . . painful wrestlings with God . . . above all . . . solitude and collectedness'. She contrasts this with the concrete and vexatious banalities of young motherhood, filled with wiping noses, bottoms or anything else leaky, multi-tasking within the household and generally being too exhausted for anything involving seeking God's face. Rather than a spiritual hierarchy privileging 'the detached life over . . . the demands and turmoils of ordinary domestic life', she claims that 'what we want is a monk who finds God while cooking a meal while one child is clamouring for a drink, another needs a bottom wiped, and a baby throws up over his shoulder'.[4]

This shows in many ways a very Ignatian instinct. For Ignatius it was about finding one's inner monastery, as it were, and taking that into whatever sector of the world one normally inhabits. There is, as the Principle and Foundation tells us, no hierarchy of life tasks that absolutely privileges one activity over another, if God is truly at the centre. At the very end of her life in 1645, during the English Civil War, Mary Ward lay dying while the Siege of York raged all around her and her whole life's work lay in ruins, destroyed by church authorities who could not accept the Ignatian way of life for women. Her vision would not be validated by those same authorities for another three centuries, but her last words ring with the confidence of someone who has learned to refer all to God in the singular freedom that is the hallmark of Ignatius himself: 'Cherish God's vocation in you. Let it be constant, efficacious and loving.'[5]

Acknowledging the gift of one's particular gifts in deep gratitude, living them out in a lifelong vocation that is faithful to its own challenges, effective in God's service for the world as it is, and enacted within a relationship of intimate love, is all the fruit one could hope for from the school of prayer of the pilgrim of Loyola.

Questions for reflection or discussion

1 How do you feel about prayer on finishing this book? Do you see a shift in the way you relate to God, yourself and the world?
2 Would you like to explore Ignatian prayer further? There are good ideas on the websites quoted in the earlier chapters. You may also like to explore the possibility of an Ignatian retreat or via the Retreat Association:

<www.jesuit.org.uk/retreats>
<www.retreats.org.uk/index.php>.

Notes

Acknowledgements

1 David L. Fleming, *Draw Me into Your Friendship: The Spiritual Exercises, a Literal Translation and a Contemporary Reading* (Institute of Jesuit Sources, Missouri, 1996), paragraph 54. (All subsequent references to the Spiritual Exercises will be from Fleming's contemporary version and referenced by paragraph, not by page, under the title of *Sp.Exx.*)

1 Getting going

1 Originally sung by soldiers in the First World War, now a football chant.
2 Thomas Merton, quoted in Douglas Burton-Christie, 'Hunger', *Spiritus* 5/2 (2005), p. vii. Available at <https://muse.jhu.edu/article/191710/pdf>.
3 *Sp.Exx.* 1.
4 Antonio Machado, *Campos de Castilla* (1912; author's own translation).

2 How it all works

1 St Richard of Chichester.
2 George A. Aschenbrenner, 'Consciousness Examen: Becoming God's Heart for the World', *Review for Religious* 47/6 (1988), pp. 801–10. You can find this article online at <http://cdm.slu.edu/cdm/singleitem/collection/rfr/id/296/rec/8>.

3 Two journeys of self-discovery

1 William Young (ed.), *Letters of St. Ignatius of Loyola* (Loyola University Press, Chicago, 1959), p. 7.
2 Joyce Huggett, 'Why Ignatian Spirituality Hooks Protestants', *The Way Supplement* (1990), pp. 22–34.
3 See <www.ignatianspiritualityproject.org/>.
4 John Morris (ed.), *The Troubles of Our Catholic Forefathers*, first to third series (London: Burns and Oates, 1877), p. 227.
5 Gillian Orchard (ed.), *Till God Will: Mary Ward through Her Writings* (Darton, Longman and Todd, London, 1985), p. 6.
6 Orchard, *Till God Will*, p. 10.
7 Orchard, *Till God Will*, p. 10.
8 *Sp.Exx.* 334.

4 The pilgrim sets out

1 John Bunyan, 'Who would true valour see'.
2 Thomas Merton, *Thoughts in Solitude* (Farrar, Straus and Giroux, New York, 1999), p. 9.
3 *Sp.Exx.* 23.
4 Henry Chadwick (ed.), *St Augustine: Confessions* (Oxford University Press, Oxford, 1991), I.i, p. 3.
5 Hildegard of Bingen, *Scivias*, 1.2.29, Classics of Western Spirituality (Paulist Press, New York, 1990), p. 117.
6 Friedrich Nietzsche, 'The Antichrist', in *The Portable Nietzsche*, ed. and trans. Walter Kaufmann (Penguin Books, New York, 1954), p. 585.
7 United Nations, *World Happiness Report* 2012.
8 St Augustine, 'Homily on the First Letter of John', 4.6.2, quoted in Christopher Jamison, *The Disciples' Call: Theologies of Vocation from Scripture to the Present Day* (T&T Clark, London, 2013), p. 88.
9 *Augustine: Confessions*, X.xxvii, p. 201.
10 Bream can be heard speaking about this on YouTube at <www.youtube.com/watch?v=0XGySXMG2GY>.

5 Who do you say I am?

1 Gerard Manley Hopkins, 'As Kingfishers Catch Fire'. This and all subsequent quotations from Gerard Manley Hopkins can be found on <www.bartleby.com>.
2 Joseph A. Munitiz and Philip Endean (eds), *Saint Ignatius of Loyola: Personal Writings* (Penguin, London, 1996), p. 24.
3 *Painted Life*, <www.congregatiojesu.org/en/maryward_painted_life.asp>, paintings 10, 11 and 30, and Christina Kenworthy-Browne (ed.), *Mary Ward (1585–1645): A Briefe Relation . . . with Autobiographical Fragments and a Selection of Letters* (Catholic Record Society, Woodbridge, 2008), pp. 76–7, 91–2.
4 Gillian Orchard (ed.), *Till God Will: Mary Ward through Her Writings* (Darton, Longman and Todd, London, 1985), p. 105.
5 Lynn White Jr, 'The Historical Roots of Our Ecological Crisis', *Science* 155/3767 (March 1967), pp. 1203–7.
6 See Adrian Del Caro and Robert Pippin (eds), *Friedrich Nietzsche: Thus Spoke Zarathustra, Second Part, On Priests* (Cambridge University Press, Cambridge, 2014), p. 71, for a closer translation of the original.
7 Gerard Manley Hopkins, 'The Wreck of the Deutschland' (l. 40).
8 See T. S. Eliot, 'The Dry Salvages', in *Four Quartets* (Faber Paperbacks, London, 1974).
9 Account given by Laínez in a letter to Juan de Polanco (1547) of experiences that Ignatius had recounted to him; taken from Jesuit historical sources.

10 Gerard Manley Hopkins, 'God's Grandeur'.
11 Thomas Aquinas, 'Adoro te devote' ('Godhead in hiding').
12 Hopkins, 'As Kingfishers Catch Fire'.
13 *Painted Life*, 21, and Orchard, *Till God Will*, p. 9.
14 Irenaeus, *Adversus Haereses* 4.34.5–7. Available online at <www.earlychurchtexts.com/public/irenaeus_glory_of_god_humanity_alive.htm>.
15 Kenworthy-Browne, *Mary Ward*, p. 122.
16 *Painted Life*, 34, and Orchard, *Till God Will*, p. 47.
17 James Walsh (ed.), *The Cloud of Unknowing* (Paulist Press, New York, 1981), ch. 75.
18 *The Revised Grail Psalms*. Copyright © 2010, Conception Abbey/The Grail, admin. by GIA Publications, Inc., www.giamusic.com. All rights reserved.
19 Stephen Mitchell (ed.), 'Saint Symeon the New Theologian, Hymn 15, We awaken in Christ's body', from *The Enlightened Heart: An Anthology of Sacred Poetry* (HarperPerennial, New York, 1993), pp. 38f.

6 The Spiritual Exercises

1 By Synesius of Cyrene (375–430), trans. W. A. Chatfield (1808–96).
2 *Sp.Exx.* 5.
3 David Hume, *Enquiries Concerning Human Understanding and Concerning the Principles of Morals*, ed. L. A. Selby-Bigge, rev. edn, P. H. Nidditch (Oxford University Press, Oxford, 1975), pp. 270–1.
4 *Sp.Exx.* 335.
5 Brian Kolodiejchuk (ed.), *Mother Teresa: Come Be My Light: The Revealing Private Writings of the Nobel Peace Prize Winner* (Doubleday, New York, 2007).

7 Caught in the system

1 W. B. Yeats, 'The Second Coming', *The Collected Poems of W. B. Yeats* (Wordsworth Poetry Library, London, 2000), p. 159.
2 Statistics based on the United Nations Sustainable Development Goals report of 2016 and related commentaries, updated in 2018. These statistics are being updated regularly and may vary.
3 Despite this being widely quoted, I have been unable to find the original source.
4 <www.dur.ac.uk/theology.religion/ccs/archives/2011/march/lecture/>.
5 Pope Francis, *Evangelii Gaudium: Apostolic Exhortation on the Proclamation of the Gospel in Today's World* (2013), 88. Available at: <http://w2.vatican.va/content/francesco/en/apost_exhortations/documents/papa-francesco_esortazione-ap_20131124_evangelii-gaudium.html>.

6 The phrase 'not less than everything' is from T. S. Eliot, 'Little Gidding', V, in *Four Quartets* (Faber Paperbacks, London, 1974), p. 59.

7 Pope Francis, 'A Big Heart Open to God', *America* magazine, 19 September 2013.

8 Pope Francis, *Evangelii Gaudium*, 49.

9 Pope Francis, *Evangelii Gaudium*, 24.

10 See Katherine Dyckman, Mary Garvin and Elizabeth Liebert, *The Spiritual Exercises Reclaimed: Uncovering Liberating Possibilities for Women* (Paulist Press, New York, 2001).

8 Surveying the wondrous cross

1 See Gemma Simmonds, 'Women Jesuits?' in Thomas Worcester (ed.), *The Cambridge Companion to the Jesuits* (Cambridge University Press, Cambridge, 2008), pp. 120–35.

2 Gillian Orchard (ed.), *Till God Will: Mary Ward through Her Writings* (Darton, Longman and Todd, London, 1985), pp. 40–1.

3 W. H. Gardner and N. H. MacKenzie (eds), *The Poems of Gerard Manley Hopkins* (Oxford University Press, Oxford, 1970), p. 90, note 1.

4 William Blake, *The Marriage of Heaven and Hell*, among the 'Didactic and Symbolical Works', in *Complete Prose of William Blake*, ed. Geoffrey Keynes (The Nonesuch Press, London, 1989), pp. 183 and 184.

5 *Sp.Exx.* 13.

9 An attitude of gratitude

1 Alexander Eaglestone, *Remembering Inigo: Glimpses of the Life of Saint Ignatius Loyola* (the *Memoriale* of Gonçalves da Câmara) (Gracewing, Leominster, 2005), p. 116.

2 Mark Mossa (ed.), *Saint Ignatius Loyola, the Spiritual Writings: Selections Annotated and Explained* (Skylight, Vermont, 2012), p. 143.

3 This well-known prayer is sometimes called 'St Teresa's bookmark' because the original, in her handwriting, was found in her breviary.

4 Fr Pedro Arrupe SJ (1907–91), 'Nothing is more practical', from *Finding God in All Things: A Marquette Prayer Book* (Marquette University, Milwaukee, WI, 2009). Used with permission.

5 De Caussade's authorship has been contested. See Dominique Salin, 'The Treatise on Abandonment to Divine Providence', *The Way* 46/2 (April 2007), pp. 21–36.

6 Tom McGuinness, 'Communion Song', *Jesuits and Friends* (Summer 2010), pp. 8–9, quoted with permission of the author.

7 Cf. Robert R. Marsh, '"I Know the Gift Can Only Be Returned": Giving and Giving Back in the *Contemplatio*', *The Way* 54/3 (July 2015), pp. 21–30.

8 The provenance of this prayer is unknown. See the article by Jack Mahoney at <www.thinkingfaith.org/articles/20120217_1.htm>.

9 Michael Ivens, *Understanding the Spiritual Exercises* (Gracewing, Leominster, 1998), p. 175.

Conclusion

1 Mark Mossa (ed.), *Saint Ignatius Loyola, the Spiritual Writings: Selections Annotated and Explained* (Skylight, Vermont, 2012), p. 221.
2 Mossa, *Saint Ignatius Loyola*, p. 243.
3 Janet Martin Soskice, 'Love and Attention' in Michael McGhee (ed.), *Philosophy, Religion and the Spiritual Life* (Cambridge University Press, Cambridge, 1992), p. 59.
4 Soskice, 'Love and Attention', pp. 61 and 62.
5 Cf. Gillian Orchard (ed.), *Till God Will: Mary Ward through Her Writings* (Darton, Longman and Todd, London, 1985), p. 121.

Copyright acknowledgements

CPSIA information can be obtained
at www.ICGtesting.com
Printed in the USA
LVHW081406291220
675328LV00029B/646

9 780281 075317